Blackmail!

Also by Arthur Black

Basic Black
Back to Black
That Old Black Magic
Arthur! Arthur!
Black by Popular Demand

Blackmail!

Exemplary Epistles,
Delightful Dispatches,
and Fanciful Faxes Sent to
"Basic Black"

Compiled by Arthur Black and Lynne Raymond

Published in 1995 by
Stoddart Publishing Co. Limited
34 Lesmill Road
Toronto, Canada
M3B 2T6
Tel. (416) 445-3333
Fax (416) 445-5967

Stoddart Books are available for bulk purchase for sales
promotions, premiums, fundraising, and seminars.
For details, contact the **Special Sales Department**
at the above address.

Canadian Cataloguing in Publication Data

Black, Arthur
Blackmail! : exemplary epistles, delightful dispatches, and
fanciful faxes sent to "basic black"

ISBN 0-7737-5765-1

1. Black, Arthur — Correspondence. I. Raymond, Lynne.
II. Title.

PS8553.L318Z54 1995   C818'.5402   C95-931220-X
PR9199.3.B53Z48 1995

Cover Design: Bill Douglas/The Bang
Computer Graphics: Tannice Goddard/S.O. Networking
Typesetting: Tony Gordon/Image One Productions Ltd.
Printed and bound in Canada

Every reasonable effort has been taken to contact authors of
these letters. Some letters have been edited for length.

*Stoddart Publishing gratefully acknowledges the support of
the Canada Council, Ontario Ministry of Citizenship,
Culture, and Recreation, Ontario Arts Council, and
Ontario Publishing Centre in the development of writing
and publishing in Canada.*

Contents

Introduction

I lied to you.

For the dozen-plus years I've been hosting my radio program, "Basic Black," I've frequently carolled on about what a marvellous means of communication radio is.

That's a crock.

"Communication" is, by definition, a two-way street. Radio, aside from the mindless blather of talk shows, is strictly one way. The hired larynx with the microphone babbles; the folks at the other end of the wire get to listen.

Fortunately, the "Basic Black" audience is far too creative to be muzzled by the shortcomings of radio technology.

They write letters. *Caramba*, do they write letters.

Away back in the early eighties, when "Basic Black" first went on the air, a few cards and letters began to trickle in. "Sure, I'll answer those," I told my producers. It was a slow afternoon. But the trickle became a freshet became a torrent became a . . .

Okay, I don't want to get carried away here. Jean Chrétien probably gets more letters than "Basic Black" does.

Let's face it, the Montreal Maroons probably still get more letters than I do.

But I wouldn't trade the 100 or so letters that pour in each week — not for a hockey stick autographed by Georges Vezina.

You are about to enjoy a smattering of the correspondence that has lightened — and enlightened — my working days over the years.

Look over my shoulder. I don't mind.

Read away.

No postage necessary.

Fauna We're Fonda . . . and Otherwise

*f*rom reptiles to raptors, from huskies to honeybees, "Basic Black" listeners spend a lot of time getting involved with various other passengers on Spaceship Earth.

Walt Whitman wrote:

I think I could turn and live with animals
They are so placid and self-contained
I stand and look at them long and long

Methinks Walt put his finger on it. There is something about the fundamental innocence of critters outside the species *Homo sapiens* that compels our respect. Or should.

The animals don't have to be massive Leviathans of the deep or burning bright tigers of Blake. As a matter of fact, we noticed particularly that an elusive little hitchhiker known to scientists as Mus musculus seemed to be popping up in our correspondence more and more often.

Or perhaps we were naturally sensitive. At the time "Basic Black" was broadcasting out of the decrepit Jarvis Street CBC studios, where it was not uncommon to have mice run over your feet — or your script.

Whatever the inspiration, we asked "Basic Black" listeners to write in with their Close Encounters of the Rodent Kind. They went for it like a you-know-what for a chunk of choice cheddar.

Dear Arthur:

First, I want to tell you that I look forward to your program each week. It's the highlight!

When my husband and I built our house eleven and a half years ago, we had a real problem with the deer mice living in the area. It would seem that they decided to move in as unpaying tenants.

The most memorable confrontation came one night after my husband left for work.

It was about 1 a.m., and I had just snuggled down in bed, when I heard a crash. I threw on my housecoat and went downstairs to check it out.

The cat had knocked the screen for my woodstove over, and a mouse was trapped underneath. I lifted the screen so that my cat could finish off the mouse, but it escaped into my dining room.

Because Oscar (the cat) had been torturing the mice, instead of killing them (I think he was tired of eating mice), I grabbed a piece of my vacuum-cleaner pipe to polish him off, if Oscar didn't.

Try to picture a person sneaking around with this "deadly weapon" raised over her head, stalking a teeny mouse.

It was cornered behind a barrel of dishes that were waiting to be unpacked. I was standing on one side, the cat on another, and the mouse on the third — like a deadly triangle.

I was poised with my arm raised, ready to strike, and slowly moved the barrel.

The cat jumped, I jumped, and the mouse ran — right between my legs. I turned to see where it had gone — it had disappeared!

The suspense didn't last long, as just a couple of seconds later I felt the mouse running up my leg, up my back, to my shoulder.

I grabbed for it under my housecoat, and couldn't reach it. So, I whipped my housecoat off, and discovered it was under my nightie! I managed to grab it, and tossed it on the floor. It then ran down the hallway, behind another carton.

It didn't escape this time; between Oscar and my pipe, we managed to "do it in."

That, incidentally, was the first time I ever killed anything other than a bug. It sure wasn't a nice feeling, but it was either him or me!

Well, keep up the good work. I can hardly wait for this Saturday, and my weekly date with you.

Debbie Sayles

January 15, 1991

Dear Arthur Black:

My most exciting encounter with a rodent occurred when I was spending Christmas holidays at my cousin's farm years ago.

The kitchen was at ground level and had a short set of steps going up to the rest of the house over the basement. The kitchen had the usual woodstove, cream separator, stand with basin and pitcher, plus a cupboard built to the floor.

A mouse got into the kitchen and we chased it with broom, mop and anything else we could lay hands on. To no avail. The call went out, "Get Pretty Kitty in here!"

When she was brought in from the barn, she understood exactly what was needed. When the mouse holed up in the cupboard, to my surprise, we were able to pull the whole thing away from the walls. Then the circus started!

The mouse and Pretty Kitty went around the circumference of the kitchen while we stood in the middle. Back of the stove, through the chair legs, behind the cupboard, 'round the separator, under the stairs, over the boots, past the door, by the slop pail, beneath the stand, back of the stove . . . about five times, until someone opened the door at just the right time. Out shot the mouse and Pretty Kitty into the snow.

With our problem solved, we shut the door, put the kitchen back in order and finished making dinner.

Yours sincerely
Frances Fryza

December 2, 1990

Dear Mr. Black:

I missed the start of your December 1 program, although I have been a faithful listener for the past several years. At any rate, when I did turn on the radio, I joined in progress your interview with the mousetrap expert; I believe his name was John Perry of Wales. My ears immediately perked up, as they have the habit of doing at the mere mention of mousetraps. No, I am not a mousetrap salesperson. Rather, it was simply a matter of stirring distant memories of a four-header mousetrap I once had. (Based on the interview, this four-header was essentially the guillotine type mentioned by Mr. Perry.)

The house in which I spent much of my childhood in Hantsport-on-the-Avon, Nova Scotia, during the 1950s, was an older house that had been built at the turn of the century by a sea captain. As kids, we were constantly poking around, and would often make fascinating discoveries in hidden nooks and crannies, not to mention abandoned root cellars and closed-off attics. One of our most treasured discoveries was an old, dirty, and colour-faded mousetrap.

It was unlike the standard mousetrap that we were accustomed to — the rectangular piece of wood with metal spring, bait holder, trip wire, and killer loop that snaps over the rodent. We had often seen and used these standard traps to catch mice who, with the onset of cool fall weather, persisted in leaving the outdoors in favour of sharing the house with us. But this old-fashioned mousetrap was unusual. It was designed to catch four mice at one setting.

The wood portion of this four-header was round in shape, approximately five inches in diameter, one inch thick, and mainly hollowed-out underneath. Its most distinctive feature were the four holes in a north-south-east-west alignment along the sides of the trap. At each hole, on the top of the trap, there was a metal spring and loop, along with a trip wire that could hold the loop in position. Bait was attached at the other end of the trip wire, and could be only approached through the hole. The loop would be pushed down inside the entrance to the hole and held in place by the trip wire.

Smelling the odour of the cheese bait, a mouse would approach, stick its head through the hole, and grab the bait. This would release the trip wire and the spring would snap up the loop. The mouse would be instantly and lethally caught at the neck or around the trunk of the body.

Hypothetically, it was possible to catch four mice at one setting. My personal record was three mice — presumably Papa Mouse, Mama Mouse, and Offspring Mouse out for a meal at a McRestaurant. Either that, or they were the three stooges of their mouse herd (pack, flock, or whatever the appropriate word is for a group of mice).

On another occasion, I forgot that I had set the trap the previous night. In fact, it was several months before I came across the trap again. When I did, it contained a mouse, or more precisely it had the skeletal remains of a mouse. The skeleton was fully intact, just like a two- or three-inch (tail not included) replica of a dinosaur in a museum.

There is really no moral or lesson to be drawn from this tale. Except perhaps, it has to do with the wisdom, or lack of it, in comments about the utility of inventing a better mousetrap.

Yours truly,
Stewart Hyson

Dear Arthur:

I have just listened to your Saturday morning stories of mice and thought you might enjoy the following saga. I have to tell you this funny story.

Chapter 1

Recently, in the Kelowna newspaper, there was a report of a man — thankfully not near my house — who went to his basement and found a strange thing wrapped around the furnace. He tried to pull it off, but it turned out to be a boa constrictor!!! (Hugging the furnace, he was!) Can you imagine?

The paper said that some three to four years ago, the house was rented to some people who bought a small boa (as a PET??). It grew; it disappeared; they moved.

Apparently it never left the house. The following day the paper reported that The Expert Snakeman in town announced that a boa was not dangerous, so no one was to worry. Please would everyone in the area put bowls of water near their furnaces and regularly check the level. If there was any change, please call him, or the S.P.C.A.

There has been no further report, but I *rush* to read the paper!

Chapter 2

When the end of the grape season came, I piled the end of my crop on a huge tray to dry for raisins for Christmas baking. I simply left it near the stove and gradually the grapes were transforming into raisins. However, two days ago, I thought I'd hurry them up a bit by putting the tray on the floor near the furnace outlet. Fine. Pulled the curtains and went to bed.

In the morning, I pulled the curtains open, glanced at the tray of grapes and saw *nothing but stems and a few dried up raisins*. No grapes, not one!!

You know the cartoon of the fellow shaking his head and scratching, rubbing his eyes? Well, I did all that. There still weren't any grapes. Horrors! My first thought was of the boa. More horrors!

Sat on the telephone stool; glanced toward the tray. Was that a tiny black speck, and another one? Six altogether. Hadn't I mopped the floor yesterday? What were they? On with the glasses. And I instantly recognized *mouse droppings!!* I've never been so thrilled and relieved in all my life.

At least it wasn't the boa!

Chapter 3

Went to the shop for mouse poison. They had sold all the gourmet bacon-and-cheese-flavoured pellets (!) but "Here is something equally good, Madam. We've had a run on mouse poison today."

I put one box on the tray with the remains of my crop, another in the basement, and went to bed.

In the morning, both boxes were completely empty! I've never encountered such hungry mice! Still not a single sign of them, dead or alive. Are they ghosts? Is it all in my head?

Chapter 4

Went to the store to buy good-old-fashioned mousetraps. The shop *was sold out!* I am not alone, entertaining mice!

Sleuthed around hunting for mouse droppings, the re-mains of mice, their door, their nest, their droppings on the stairway — nothing. Only six mouse droppings.

Two hours later; I had mousetraps and mouse seed everywhere: on the tray with its remaining stems and raisins, under the stove, near the assumed entrance. It was just like summer camp!

There is no conclusion to the final chapter but one month after the story was first reported, boa "Mungo" has been identified by its original owner, a young boy. He says: "He's harmless; used to curl up in bed with us, and lie on the back of the couch and play with the cat . . ."

Shall I send you the conclusion when and if there is one?

Sincerely,
Cynthia Ellis

June 9, 1991

Dear Arthur:

I did not catch the phone numbers quickly enough to phone in my pet adventure story. So here it is.

When I was a little girl in Montreal, we (my brother and sisters and I) had mice as pets. They were prolific breeders. We kept some of the baby mice as pets. The rest we took to a pet shop in downtown Montreal. This being the '70s, we named one of our pets "Pierre Elliott Trudeau." He turned out to be the fiercest, nastiest, most womanizing mouse that we had ever had. He was so mean that it was decided he had to go. So, on our next expedition to the pet store, Pierre E. came with us.

The trip was undertaken on the Metro. We had the mice in boxes: the boy mice in one box, and the girl mice in another. The boxes were open, with wire screen on top. On the Metro, Pierre E. managed to wriggle out of the boys' box. Had he run away from us, who knows what adventures he could have had, with the entire Metro system as his domain? Fortunately, he was easy to recapture, as he went straight for the girls' box and tried to chew his way in!

I wonder what ever became of him?

Sincerely,
Jean Rath

Dear Arthur:

Okay, okay — one more mouse story! I missed the show that first aired these stories, so I'm a little late with this.

This happened the summer before last, when we found a nest of four tiny little mice, which we brought into the house as pets (at the same time we had been waging war with mouse-traps and cat on the adults of this species living in our walls . . .). Our four-year-old daughter, whose favourite pas-time is pretending to be a cat, was of course constantly showering attention on them. One day we were out in the yard when Amelia came running out of the house, hiding something in her hand, and into the woods where she threw something down and came running back. Upon investigation we found a dead mouse. When we questioned her, she said she had been pretending to be a cat and had bitten the mouse! She later changed the story twice, saying she had squished it, and then that she had drowned it in the water dish. Whatever the truth was, the result was one dead mouse and an unrepentant child (she *was* a cat after all, and so felt no remorse). We set the other three mice free shortly afterwards — we thought their survival chances better outdoors than in a house with an over-grown two-legged "cat." Then again, there's nothing to say that the little carcasses I pulled out of my mousetraps in the following months weren't the same little creatures I had tried to make pets of.

May you forever survive the budget cuts — we love your show!

Diane, Cyril and Amelia

Dear Sir:

My wife and I listened with slight dismay (although not too great — because it really doesn't matter) to your disinformation program about geckos on two recent broadcasts. Not even your correspondent in Kingston really understands geckos. We have lived with them for twenty-five years (as medical missionaries in Irian Jaya, Indonesia). Let me add some firsthand information.

We first met geckos the evening of our first day in the warm tropics, as they clambered up the outside of the screened window to catch insects attracted by the inside lights in our room. The gecko would wait patiently until a moth landed, then stealthily creep within striking distance and presto! — catch the insect in its mouth and devour it. It was interesting to see the struggle if the insect was too big for the gecko.

It became a problem when our little reptilian visitors got inside the house. They did eat some insects, although very few cockroaches; but one often found a crevice behind a light fixture on the ceiling over my desk in which to hide during the daytime hours and digest last night's catch. Not infrequently, a letter (perhaps to some important government office) left exposed on the desk was nicely struck dead centre by a neat blob of chichak droppings. Yes, we called them "chi-chucks" — a much better name, because it sounds like the noise they make. You said geckos don't bark. Not so. We often heard them calling back and forth with their loud "chi-chi-chi-chi-chi" cry. And they laid their eggs indiscriminately in any convenient undisturbed spot in the place — such as inside light switches, the linen cupboard or a tool box. We often couldn't figure how they got in to deposit their little 1-cm crackly-shelled white eggs.

The biggest problem a gecko ever caused me came one night about 2 a.m. We had an old-fashioned crank telephone system linking our home with several other residences, the health centre and the maternity ward. I was awakened by the phone — but when I picked it up no one was there. I went back to bed, but it soon tinkled again. Still no one on the other end. I figured that one of the village midwives who didn't know how to use the phone might be calling for help. So I got up and went over to the labour ward. Darkness. No one there. The health centre was also quiet. Soon I was back in bed, and the phone rang again. So I cranked out a long loud ring on our party line system, awakening everyone to ask if all was well. Our phone was our distress line in case anyone had a problem. One house didn't answer, so I plodded over there to wake them up and discovered that they, as well as everyone else, had been sleeping undisturbed (until I came along). I went home again and stuffed a sock between the clapper and the bells on the phone box and slept quietly until dawn.

In the morning I attacked the phone box with a screwdriver. Inside — a large gecko who obviously had been doing his exercises beside the clapper rod, ringing the bells loudly enough to waken me. I then attacked him — and it was a more successful attack than I have sometimes made on geckos. If you catch a gecko by the tail, it can easily snap off its tail, leaving it writhing convulsively in your hand as the rest of friend gecko scurries off to regrow another.

My advice — don't introduce geckos for cockroach control. One of my friends brought them into an isolated area in Irian Jaya, where, oddly enough, there had not been any, to control spiders. It didn't work. In my experience they don't seem to reduce the cockroach population much. If there were no other insects they might eat a few. But it sure isn't a sure solution to the problem.

Yours truly,
C. K. Dresser, M.D.

Dear Mr. Black:

I am a watch officer on a 111' wooden square-top sail schooner called the *Pacific Swift* of Victoria, B.C. The *Swift* is used as a sail training vessel for teenagers and young adults. She has twice sailed to the South Pacific. What is one of the inevitable results of visiting the islands of French Polynesia, Samoa and Tonga?? . . . COCKROACHES! At the end of the *Swift*'s maiden voyage to Australia we had an exterminator come to bomb the boat and he said the *Swift* was the worst case he had seen in over twenty years of dealing with the critters. We tried a gecko but he disappeared when the weather got cold in the northern climes.

Could you please send me the words to "Gecko in the Night," the song you played on your show this morning. It would help us to ease the fears of young lady trainees who tend to react rather violently to finding roaches scuttling over their pillows at night, hiding under the rims of their mugs, feasting on the remnants of hot chocolate from the night before, or falling from the beams into their soup at lunch.

I have enclosed one of our brochures to give you a better idea of what we are all about, and yes, despite our unwanted stowaways, we have unlimited fun and excitement plying the ocean coastally and abroad.

Sincerely,
Dorothy Jones

March 9, 1991

Dear Arthur:

I have been a regular listener to your Saturday morning program for a number of years, and have really enjoyed the material that you present. Until now, I have not had the occasion or opportunity to write to you.

What finally got me around to this letter was a little gem of a song that I heard on your program this morning just after 11:00 a.m. local (MST) time, as broadcast on CBC's Windermere Valley, B.C., FM network. We have a home in Windermere and spend a lot of time there.

The song referred to was titled "Gecko in the Night." It really caught my interest and tickled my funny bone as we have recently returned from a month's vacation on the island of Maui, Hawaii. In the condominium we stayed in we had at least four resident geckos — one that sneaked around our bedroom at night, one that seemed to take care of the living room, another that found a temporary home inside the light fixture outside the front door, and another that we didn't ever see, but it "chirped" quite loudly and very happily from somewhere up in the open-beam ceiling in the living room. My wife and I, and two other Canadian couples who shared our Maui home for parts of our stay, all got quite attached to our little gecko friends, and thought of them as pets. They are extremely well thought of in the islands, as you may know, and, in fact, our condominium instructions were very clear in that the geckos were much-appreciated guests and should on no account be injured or disturbed.

Anyway, I really got a kick out of the song, and wondered if I could get a copy of it, so that I can share the song with our guests. I know they would enjoy it as much as I did. I hope you can help me with this, and look forward keenly to your reply. Meanwhile, keep up the good work with your program and our best wishes for continued success.

Yours very truly,
Ken and Irene Lloyd

February 10, 1991

Dear Arthur:

Your "gecko" piece on "Basic Black" on February 9 brought back my own memories, or shall I say run-ins, with geckos in Indonesia last year.

Picture this. Aili (pronounced I-lee) and I were sleeping soundly in our room at an inn in Ubud (oo-bood), Bali — and then it started. A lone gecko screaming "Gecko" (or we thought it sounded like screaming) at the top of its lungs. We did not know where the noise was coming from. From our bed, under our bed, the ceiling, the wall — a frantic search revealed nothing (besides, at 2 in the morning how focused are you?). After about fifteen minutes the calling stopped and it was quiet for the remainder of the night. Next night the same thing, but this time it was much less of a surprise. By the third night, New Year's Eve, we were ready. We would not go to bed until after the calling — besides, we were still up so it made no difference. And wouldn't you know it? Our beloved gecko only made one quick gecko "chirp" and was never heard from again. We never did see our little friend but our days in Ubud would not have been the same.

Arthur, I have but one request. Please play "Gecko in the Night" just once more.

Sincerely,
Heidi Klein

Dear Arthur:

I am mailing to you a story about my cockatiel bird, Howie. I listen to your show every Saturday, and thought that maybe if you were interested you could tell my story.

I admit it is a bit corny, but it is fascinating how one little bird could cause so much trouble in my life.

Howie the Cockatiel

This is a strange but very true love story. Howie was once only my pet cockatiel, but now he is *everyone's* pet.

Let me explain . . . my husband and I purchased Howie for only $24.00 at the annual Bird Auction held every October in Pembroke, Ontario. We didn't really need another bird; we already had two budgies, Miss Blue and Elvis. But then again my husband Ed can't resist a bargain. So, Howie came home with us that day.

At first we named him Marge but after his first check-up with the veterinarian he came home to be renamed Howie. Howie grew to be a loving pet, too loving in a lot of cases. Howie was indeed my bird and shadow. After just a few short weeks he followed me *everywhere* . . . he was kept in his cage only at night, and would only go inside himself for a nap or to eat. He was so smart that he could identify the sound of my footsteps when I got out of bed in the morning. Ed could be up for hours and Howie would just snooze under his blanket, but as soon as my feet would hit the carpet he would start with his "squeaking." Out he would fly, right to me, and away we would go for the day. If I had a shower, he had one too. He would sit on my shoulder and face away from the spray, or jump down to the edge of the bathtub and be sprayed lightly. He loved the whirlpool bath, and would try and catch the bubbles going by. More than a few times he jumped right in with me. He was very unique: if I decided I wanted to sleep in on a Sunday morning, Howie would become impatient waiting for me to get up, so he would shriek until I got out of bed, took him out and carried him back to bed with me. There he would sit on top of a little Kleenex, which was on top of my tummy, and he would sleep until I got up, no matter what the hour. At times he was a bit of a voyeur and this drove my husband mad.

Nothing in our home frightened Howie. Even in Ed's workshop he would get onto the table saw and go for a ride. He was also intrigued by the typewriter and would like to sit on the roller like he was balancing on a log.

When we would go down to Brantford to visit my mother, Howie would come with us. He would get out of the cage and he would settle on my shoulder for the length of the drive just looking at the view. If you have noticed, I have been using the past tense when talking about Howie. Well, in a sense he is in the past. Oh, he is alive and he is once again with me, but he is indeed a rare bird.

What do I mean? Well, on June the twelfth my husband went out to get the mail, and Howie went out with him. He flew straight as an arrow nonstop into the woods in front of our home. I was not home at the time, I was in Brantford, where my mother was having surgery, a 500-km journey. I wondered why my husband was not answering our phone. I was calling to let him know my mom was okay, and time and time again there was no response. He finally phoned me late in the evening to tell me about Howie, how he escaped and how he could not be found. He had searched all day. I instantly broke into tears and if I could have I would have spread my wings and flown the six hours back to Petawawa to find him. Instead I had to wait until the morning. I packed up and left at 05:00 hours for Petawawa, certainly the longest drive of my life. Once I got back to Petawawa I began my search. The search lasted six weeks, six long and painful weeks.

We live in a small community. My husband is with the Canadian Armed Forces on the base at Petawawa, and we live in the village, a population of 4,500. The military base itself is only 2 km away from the village.

At the time I was taking a full-time French course and was able to take time off to look for Howie. And look I did! I posted wanted signs all over the base and the village itself. I rented a sign and put it out on Highway 17. I placed ads in the *Petawawa Post* and *Pembroke Observer*, and even as far away as Ottawa. It didn't take long before I received calls from people all over "supposedly" seeing Howie everywhere. With every call I got I checked it out. I could go on and on about the calls, but I will let you in on just a few. One of the first calls I received was from a little girl who said she saw Howie in her backyard. I raced over to the address to find a girl about ten years old waiting for me. I asked her to describe the bird and she did. But what she described was a green budgie. It was shortly after that I came across a family who had lost that budgie two weeks before. I knew that if that little budgie could survive so could my Howie.

Howie is a white cockatiel with bright orange cheeks and a yellow crest. A lady called and reported finding white feathers under her bird feeder, so over I went: once again a false lead. I even received a call at 11:30 in the evening from a security guard, a soldier doing rounds on the base. He was a little embarrassed to be calling me that late in the evening, but I vaulted into my Tercel and raced over to find him waiting for me. My husband was in bed with a broken toe and fast asleep so I went without him. In any other community I would have hesitated to leave at that hour but Petawawa is relatively safe. So, here I was, near midnight, with a strange man, two flash-lights and two people intent on finding this white cockatiel. He said he observed the bird under a tree pecking at the ground and when he realized that it might be "the" bird he went out of his way to find my telephone number and call me. We looked and called "Howie" for one and a half hours. You might ask what a bird would be doing eating at that hour; well, Howie being so exotic-looking would have to be very careful about how and when he ate, as he was a target for all the other birds in the neighbourhood. When Howie returned six weeks later he was found to have calluses on the bottom of his feet from being "holed" up in one spot for so long. Anyway, the soldier and I had little success and I arrived home at 01:00 hours.

It appears that Howie spent an abundant amount of his time on the golf course. At least that is where he was spotted the most. I went as far as putting a cage right down on the course, and leaving little bags of birdseed in the clubhouse. Petawawa is a very nice place to live indeed; that cage sat there for ten days and not a soul moved it. A number of packages of seeds were taken as a "just-in-case" by the golfers. I really appreciated that and I sent a thank-you note to the clubhouse this spring. Where else would people be so co-operative and helpful? Canadian Forces families are the greatest!

We had a number of telephone calls as well. Some smart aleck called and told me that he found Howie but was very sorry as he had just had him for a barbecue, and *not* as the guest. Someone called and, imitating an oriental accent, told me that he was calling from the Crescent Gardens (restaurant) and that Howie was found but was now in the duck soup. Mostly people were very considerate and we received many phone calls asking if we had found him. Even the prank caller phoned back and said that he really hoped that we would find him.

When it came time for Ed and I to go on vacation we left with heavy hearts. It had been four weeks and still Howie had not been unearthed. No one had called in days with any sightings and I felt that he had become too frail to continue. You see, cockatiel birds are originally from Australia and they do not have any homing sense whatsoever. In Australia, where there isn't a lot of fresh water inland, the birds fly constantly in search of water. The only time they have a homing sense is nesting time. So even if Howie wanted to find his way home he couldn't.

So, we left for a week-long houseboating vacation. I called my friend Bella Conroy every other day to see if there had been any calls, and there hadn't. The day after our houseboat vacation ended we were on a plane on our way to Las Vegas. Once again I called Bella, this time from casinos, and still no Howie. We returned from Las Vegas to Brantford to find a message on my mother's answering machine. We were to call Bella right away, and we did. Sure enough, she had in her possession one rough-looking white cockatiel. It was much too late for us to drive the six hours home so we left first thing in the morning. I was so nervous; what if it wasn't my Howie?

Who had found him and where? Elizabeth Fry, a photographer from the base *Post* newspaper, found him in her backyard. Only two miles from our home. He was too weak to fly, so didn't prove too laborious to catch. He did however inflict painful bites on her. She called my home and heard the message to call Bella, and thankfully she did. (I rewarded her with $100.00.)

Well, we arrived in Petawawa at noon, straight to Bella's and there he was, one sick, bleeding, featherless Howie. Our Howie hit our ceiling fan just before he flew away from home and he had a dent in his beak; sure enough so did this cockatiel. We took him directly to the vets in Pembroke, but they are not bird specialists, and there wasn't much they could do. We then drove the 13-km trip to Ottawa to Bells Corners Animal Hospital where they have a lot of experience with exotic birds. He was cleaned up and we were given lessons on how to inject an antibiotic into him. We had to give him needles twice a day, not an easy task for someone who doesn't like receiving needles herself. We did get the needle-giving down to an art though. Howie had a very rough time. He had been attacked by other birds and was suffering from a large bloody gash on his back and one under his wing. He had only one tail feather, not the usual fourteen. He was definitely underweight, and worst of all he wasn't glad to see me, at least he didn't even appear to know me. I was so hurt!

In the beginning of this story I told you what a wonderful pet Howie was, but unfortunately all the suffering he endured while away for six weeks took its toll. Howie, when he was physically better, refused to fly. I guess that was because each time he did, he was attacked, so he walked everywhere instead. My husband built him a four-foot ladder so he could come out of his cage for exercise by climbing up to a wall perch we have for him. He is over that now, but it had taken him three months to fly again. Another thing that Howie changed was his love for water. I used to have to shoo him away from the sink when I was doing dishes. There were several times when he decided to jump right into the suds when my back was turned and he had to be rescued. But I suppose being out in the heavy rains turned him off showers altogether. Now when the other birds have a shower with my plant mister he runs for cover.

I felt sorry for him; before he left home he would have nothing to do with the two budgies, but now that he was back he was climbing into their cage with them and sleeping at night. It was very funny to see this huge bird cuddled up with the budgies in a small cage. So I bought him a girlfriend. Her name is Iris and she is a grey cockatiel. At first it was not love at first sight. Howie was scared to death of her, but finally like any male he gave in to her ways. Howie and Iris are inseparable now, which I am happy for . . . but Howie unfortunately will not be my pet ever again. He hates to be touched, and I swear he is hard of hearing. Just the same, I still love him.

Howie has made a celebrity of me, and I still can't go anywhere without someone asking me how he is. I don't mind much, but I still get introduced as Howie's mom and then I have to tell this tale of Howie once again. It is indeed a tragic story, but at least now I can say I know where Howie spends his evenings.

Oh, and one last bit of news: Iris and Howie are expectant parents! Iris has laid five eggs in the last week. She is being a good mom and Howie is doing his share. Maybe, just maybe, I will have five little cockatiels squeaking out Howie's name. He will then for sure have a reason to stay home!

Yours truly,
Marny Forrest

P.S. She actually laid six eggs in total.

February 16, 1991

Dear Arthur:

As always, I enjoyed your show this morning, Saturday 16th.
My excuse for this is because I have a parrot story for you.

A dear old lady was given a pet parrot, but soon discovered
that it swore dreadfully. She tried everything she could think
of to stop the Fowl Language (sorry!) but still the bird swore.
Finally she told the bird it would be put in the freezer for a
spell if it swore again. It soon did, and she popped it into the
freezer, and took it out after about ten minutes.

The poor creature sat shivering and finally managed to
speak.

"Hey," it said. "What did the *turkey* in there do?!"

Sincerely,
Irene

Dear Arthur:

I've just finished listening to your program on "Living Things We Love to Hate." At first I thought the subject was my ex-husband but was even more disillusioned with you when it turned out to be his kindred spirit, the slug. It reminded me, right off, of a wonderful painting of a snail called *Two Million Years of Spinelessness* which sent me into unrestrained hilarity in a library as quiet as a tomb. Oh — back to my thought — he really is scraping the bottom of the rain barrel so to speak. Arthur needs some encouragement — perhaps even an idea or two. So here's a good one. Just prior to Christmas I agreed to give a home to a stray dog, sight unseen. She had a pathetic story behind her and I do love underdogs. I hadn't owned a "mixed breed" in my life, and was amazed at so many perfect strangers launching into conversations praising the mixed breed — which hitherto I had called a plain mutt, but wouldn't dare now! Even the vet sang their praises when we saw her. They have, I realize, a large loyal band of followers who wouldn't dream of owning anything else.

So during the January sales, I was in a book store and immediately spied on the sale table a book called *Intelligent and Loyal* written by Jilly Cooper, an English journalist, in praise of the "mixed breed." It was full of funny, sad, heroic doggy tales. She (Jilly) is smart and amusing and I'm sure you'd enjoy a chat with her; do consider it. It would be several rungs up the ladder from slugs — and I don't just mean the evolutionary ladder. I'm sorry I can't give you any other details —

33

needless to say I lent the book out to another dog lover — but I'm sure another W. H. Smith will be able to find one for you.

A regular listener,
Janice Delaney

P.S. Your postcard looks most handsome on my refrigerator. If you don't mind my saying, you are more attractive than your voice. I was expecting the opposite as that's what's usually true of radio personalities!

September 29, 1990

Dear Arthur:

Further to your discussion of pets bonding to the interloping infant.

We got our female Airedale in April. In June she was still a gangly puppy when we brought our daughter home from the hospital. The first night we sent Ginger to her bed and settled our brand new daughter Jennifer into her infant crib. When I got up in the early morning to a summons from Jennifer, there was Ginger asleep on the floor at the foot of Jen's infant crib.

Thereafter, whenever I would put Jennifer in her carriage outside in the yard, Ginger would plant herself by the carriage and "baby-sit" her charge.

I guess the writing was on the wall. Whenever Ginger would occasionally disappear we usually found her either at the park or in the school yard with the kids.

Incidentally, when it was Ginger's turn to have babies — puppies — she was a caring and solicitous mom as well.

Sincerely,
Jean Greenough

January 22, 1990

Dear Arthur Black:

As a fan of yours for several years, I enjoyed your program
(as always) on January 20th, especially the selections of dog
stories. I thought I would share with you a dog story of my own.

This story is about my dog Kluane, a tall, tan, but stupid
husky I entertained while growing up in Whitehorse, Yukon.
One summer, when the salmon were running, I decided to join
a friend and his family out at Dalton Post, a small fishing spot
about 150 miles southwest of Whitehorse.

After work one Saturday, I piled my gear and Kluane into
my Jeep and set off from Dalton Post. I arrived late at night,
found my friend's family camp, and joined the traditional
Yukon pre-fishing festivities. Needless to say, dawn broke early
the next morning, and after a few cups of coffee we all set out
for the river. The hike, over rocky, rootbound trails, lasted for
nearly two miles, and of course the only one to really enjoy it
was Kluane. Finally we came upon the river, set in a low
wooded gully, and began to descend to its bank.

Suddenly, Kluane broke away from us and ran towards the
river. She jumped into the water, swam to the opposite side,
and clambered up the bank, startling a porcupine. Having
never seen a porcupine before, she did to it what she always
did when confronting small rodents, human arms or unpro-
tected furniture: she sank her teeth into the animal, shook it
around and then threw it into the nearby bushes, apparently
none the worse for wear. It immediately scurried away.

Now, there is of course a reason why porcupines move slowly, without much care. That reason amounted to a little over seventy-five quills stuck into Kluane's snoot, protruding at crazy angles. Without even so much as dipping my lure into the water, I turned around, marched through the brush back to my Jeep, and drove the 150 miles to Whitehorse, where I had to pay a veterinarian overtime to remove the quills from Kluane's mouth.

Without a doubt, that was simultaneously the most expensive and shortest fishing trip I have ever had.

Doggedly yours,
Randy Germain

January 20, 1990

Dear Mr. Black:

Would you, I wonder, be interested in the following enclosure? It is a true pet story which happened when we lived in rural Napanee.

The Rescue

Years ago when first married it was difficult to find a place to live.

Finally an elderly bachelor rented us three downstairs rooms in his old farmhouse.

My husband worked nights. Soon I slept uneasily due to strange noises under my bedroom windows. Peeping Toms? I was truly afraid.

Rising early one morning I saw a large red collie dog get-ting up from one of the holes he'd dug under my bedroom windows.

He was a beautiful dog but, lacking the long nose of the purebreds, had seemingly been crossbred once.

At first we tried vainly to find his owner. Then it became apparent that he had been not only abandoned but also shut up and beaten.

So I adopted him, or rather he adopted me. He refused to be parted from me. Everywhere I went he went and lay at my feet.

I taught him many tricks. He *wanted* to learn.

When winter came he took me for many long sled rides.

One afternoon he stalled at the top of a steep hill. I insisted so we started down. The hill proved, unexpectedly, to be very icy. Halfway down — I'll never know why — I looked behind. A huge milk truck was almost upon us.

Scarcely had the thought flashed through my mind, *Red's only a pup, I can't stop, the truck can't,* when I found myself landed sideways in a big snowbank as the truck crashed by! Thankfully I got up and hugged and hugged "My Red."

I learned two things that afternoon:

1. Never to go where he was reluctant to go.
2. The snow-sounds are not easily heard by *human* ears.

Yours truly,
Ethel McNeill

January 17, 1990

Dear Arthur:

Re: Pet Story

I phoned your answering machine — too late! A human voice replied, so I'll tell you this doggy tale this way.

In 1953 I was posted to the Northwest Highway System, first at Whitehorse, later at Dawson. In Dawson in 1954 I acquired a male springer spaniel from a litter born in Whitehorse (a Major Whalley presided!). So "Danny" came with us to Chilliwack and on a 13,000-mile car and camping trip across the U.S. to Fort Belvoire, Virginia (Marine Training Base at Camp LeJuene), the only dog to climb the tower at Gettysburg National Cemetery! Then to Florida — Georgia — Louisiana — Texas — New Mexico (he kept us awake, barking from the tent opening at silhouetted cactus on the distant hill, probably thought they were bandits). To Nevada, Arizona, etc., and return to Chilliwack.

In 1959 he came on our final posting to Ottawa and back as a civilian to Vancouver in 1961. To Quesnel then to Kamloops in 1963. He sired a pup, "Dagmar," just before we left Quesnel. Dagmar stayed.

Then in 1965 he flew with us to Uganda, East Africa. I took a position with External Aid (later CIDA), as an engineering advisor to Obote's Ugandan government. So here was our beloved pet, in the tropics and faced with weekly creosote dips to keep the ticks at bay. In 1966 poor old Danny's heart gave out and at the age of fifteen he passed on. Born in Whitehorse, died in Kampala, Uganda! We still miss him.

Al & Willma Slater

Dear Arthur:

This morning, heard your request for call-in stories of wild-animal encounters. My only encounters involve sightings, but my son had some interesting experiences one summer doing exploration for a mining company in the Yukon.

It was the first wilderness living for Russ and Larry. The boys were deposited by helicopter in different locations every week. Were told they would see caribou but that was no problem, caribou just curious creatures; however, a rifle part of the basic gear, something neither familiar with.

The first morning, as they made their way to base of this particular mountain, noticed eleven caribou . . . the boys continued up the slope . . . to their surprise, upon reaching the crest, discovered the caribou had circled around and come up the far side, now standing in a circle staring at the intruders.

Russ said, although we were told caribou just curious, seeing them *en masse* somewhat intimidating. Larry took off along the ridge, while Russ decide to return down the slope . . . only to realize the caribou in hot pursuit. It was obvious no way could he outrun the caribou, so stopped and turned to face them . . . on came the caribou to within fifty yards of where he stood, then stopped in their tracks. A few minutes later, the large bull gave a whistle and back up the slope they galloped . . . obviously satisfied they'd had their "sport" with the intruder into their territory!

Camped by a small lake, they had a morning and evening visit from one of the little beavers who lived in the lodge out in the lake. The little fellow just sat and observed these two "strange beings" — obviously baby beaver's first encounter with same.

Then there was the morning Russ was setting up the survey tripod, in front of their camp — turned to speak to Larry busy making breakfast. When Russ turned back to his surveying, discovered a large grizzly was "surveying" him. Larry fetched the rifle, hoping this might intimidate the uninvited visitor . . . then began the waiting game . . . Russ said he had no idea they had such a massive head. No way of knowing what the bear was making of them being there . . . but after a couple of minutes (that seemed like eternity) . . . gave a grunt and continued its way around base of mountain.

Sincerely,
Lee Davis

January 31, 1991

Dear Arthur:

I'm a fan of your show and listen to it when I can.

Several weeks ago I heard one of the rodent/rat stories you've narrated and it prompted me to write the little note I enclosed.

Keep up the good work, Art!

As a male growing up in the late fifties and sixties in a fairly typical Canadian household, one of my jobs was to take out the garbage. Our family occupied the main floor of the house and rented out two small basement suites. With the additional people in the house we required four garbage cans which were situated underneath our back porch.

One day as I was about to put the garbage into a can I was startled by a large rat leaping out as I pulled off a loosely fitting lid. In the oral history that little boys tell each other aren't there always stories of large and vicious rats? Big bold rats that turn on cats, drive away dogs and even attack people if cornered. I heard plenty of stories like this.

Given my nature and temperament, which predisposes me to flight rather than fight, and a good imagination focusing on vicious rat stories, for me, taking out the garbage took on an element of risking life and limb. The fact that the first rat had proved to be cowardly was no guarantee that the next one would not match the mythology. I had visions of large rats disturbed at their meal, leaping out of a garbage can to attach themselves to my throat.

Defensive measures were called for to counter this threat. Now whenever I took out the garbage, going down the back stairs I would walk slowly, stomp my feet loudly and give a couple of good hollers. Just in case a brave rat had found food worth fighting for, or a tough old rat with a hearing problem was still in a can, I would snatch off the lid and leap back in one motion. If necessary the lid in my hand could be used as a shield to ward off a throat-seeking rat missile. These techniques were highly successful and for several weeks I neither saw nor heard a rat.

Then one day as I stepped out on the back porch, garbage bag in hand and ear cocked for danger, I heard the unmistakable sound of a garbage can lid moving. Instantly I sprang into frenzied action. Leaning over the porch rail I hollered at the top of my voice down towards the garbage cans while my feet galloped a thundering tattoo on the porch floor. After several seconds my technique was successful and I stood face to face with the enemy. From beneath the porch appeared the bewildered and puzzled face of our basement suite tenant, Mr. Walter Plaviuk, who stood gazing up at me, holding an empty garbage pail. "What the hell is going on?" he said, or words to that effect.

I looked down at him feeling very embarrassed and sheepishly mumbled something about thinking he was a rat.

Without requiring further explanation Mr. Plaviuk turned his back on me and returned to his apartment. After that I varied my rat defence techniques somewhat to avoid a similar occurrence. I never did see another rat in our garbage cans.

A loyal fan,
Arthur Peters

Dear Arthur:

Yesterday you asked your listeners to write about unusual things their animals had done. I've had two cats that I would think fit that category.

Tink loved travelling. As soon as he heard the car door open, he would come running. When I had to take a bus trip, I would open my flight bag and Tink would hop in. With space left for his nose to breathe, he was perfectly content. I have taken him on a ten-hour bus trip, and on numerous ferry crossings, just holding the bag. He never gave a sign that he was in the flight bag.

My other cat, Billy, loved to sit on the back porch, and always seemed to be on or around it. Then he started to disappear from the porch — and I didn't have a clue where he had gone. One day I happened to be looking out the window, and saw him purposefully trotting toward a tangle of brush near my backdoor neighbours. A few minutes later I saw a female cat who had been pregnant (but was obviously no longer that way) scoot out of the bushes. Impelled by curiosity, I walked over to see what was going on. Billy had become a baby-sitter! Five furry little shapes were just learning the joys of getting away from the nest. Billy would carefully go after the wanderers, pick them up by the scruff of their necks, and return them to the nest, where he would stretch out beside them. After some time, Mamma Cat returned, obviously refreshed and having enjoyed her time away from her constant attention-seekers. Billy, the surrogate mother, trotted happily to my back porch. This happened numerous times. When things became just too much for Mother Cat to bear, she meowed for Billy to come and baby-sit while she had a little time off! This was made even stranger by the fact that Billy couldn't possibly have been the father — he was a neutered male.

I read one of your articles in our local paper and was pleased to see that you write just as you talk. Here's hoping I'm the lucky one who gets a copy of *Basic Black*.

Sincerely,
Kathleen Ten Wolde

Dear Arthur:

I was about to start this letter by telling you that all my (your) books had been stolen or borrowed and not returned (I do have two of your books) so that I might possibly receive a copy of *Arthur! Arthur!*, which I don't have. But I thought the following anecdote might catch your literary "eye." I have taken poetic licence but the following is much like it *could* have happened.

I felt great as I had most of my Christmas gifts bought and wrapped and only had some fabric stencilling left to do.

Humming softly as I prepared the fabric, I eyed my cat Too-Too contentedly catnapping on the high stool by the table. She had a habit of sleeping with one eye open. I never could tell if she was sleeping or just keeping an eye on things.

The phone rang. I wondered whether to answer it. Having just begun my work, I decided to answer it. Unfortunately, this was a mistake. It was one of those "I'll save you money" calls. I said that I wasn't interested and hung up.

I returned to the kitchen. My stencilling had already been done for me. Too-Too was no longer catnapping. She was walking all over the fabric. This would have been fine but she had knocked over a red paint jar and some had fallen into a tray. Her red paw prints were placed strategically (?) all over the fabric. I was furious but knew never to hit a cat. I carefully carried her to the sink and washed her paws — needless to say, with much struggle!

After cooling off and giving my furry companion an equally

cold stare, I went back to my fabric. I examined it and thought to scrap it, but instead hung it up to dry to set the paint. My mother always said "Haste makes waste." She was right. A week later, I had all of my Christmas gifts made, oven mitts, serviettes, headbands et al. printed with my own Too-Too's paws!

I hope you will enjoy this as much as I enjoyed writing it. I hope this won't go *in* the *out* basket before it's read (red — pun on words)!

Yours very truly,
Sherlee Aho

Dear Arthur:

On your September 29th program you invited listeners to recount adventures which highlighted their lives. I immediately thought of the moment when I was confronted by a lion in the woodlands of northeastern Zambia.

In the mid-seventies, I was one of about thirty Canadians who participated in a CIDA contract to manage Zambia Railways. Near the end of my two years there, I went on a week-long walking safari in Luangua National Park. Every day a guide led our party of five tourists on foot through the woodlands to view the wildlife. The hike took us between campsites where we slept in tents overnight.

One night our sleep was interrupted by the roaring and growling of lions. At dawn, before breakfast, the guide took us to investigate the cause of the night's activities. Soon we encountered the carcass of an infant elephant which had been "taken" by the lions. Our group swung back toward camp. As we threaded our way through large clumps of bushes beside a dry streambed, a lion jumped out. The guide raised and readied his rifle as I reached for my camera . . .

But then I thought, this wasn't adventurous Art. I had a guide ahead of me and a guard behind me — both with high-powered rifles. If anything was having an adventure, it was the lion.

Maybe I had an adventure when one-ton hippopotamuses were grazing around my tent at night at Chunga campground in Kafue National Park? But then, I didn't really see the hippos — just the crushed grass.

No, Arthur, I guess I was REALLY having an adventure when I was stranded alone on the Busanga Plain by a large, toothy elephant. On an afternoon of a camping trip in Kafue National Park, I was slowly cruising the dirt roads of the park looking for wildlife. I decided to try the road on the Busanga Plain which dead-ended at a water hole. A likely place for animals to congregate. At the water hole I saw some zebras and wildebeests. I turned my car and started back. I hadn't gone far when I saw an elephant approaching straight down the middle of the track! There was nowhere to escape to the rear. My car couldn't go far across the rough plain. There were no trees to climb.

Slowly, I drove toward the huge beast. When only a couple of hundred feet separated us, the elephant suddenly turned aside into the grass. That was enough adventure for one so I hastily fled back to camp!

Yours truly,
Derek Wilson

January 12, 1991

Dear Arthur:

We listen to your program every Saturday and today is no exception. We love it. Today, I'm recovering from a nasty cold, snuggled in an old quilt on the sofa, allowing your interesting monologue to lessen my personal ills.

Furred Friends stories? I have one for you. Not a mouse story but a brown bear story. We frequently have bears visit our yard during the summer to check out our compost box, which we are used to by now, and we respect their space and usually they more or less respect ours, except for one bear. This one decided it was time for a change of wardrobe and would pull clothes off of my clothesline, walking over and dragging the items around the yard. This we considered to be a definite infringement so called the Forestry Department to bring a bear tank trap. The wildlife officer just could not resist asking what kind of wearing apparel the bear seemed to prefer. He laughed heartily when I told him the bear was quite selective, only taking my skirts and blouses. A pale green skirt was a definite favourite. We didn't catch the bear in our yard. She/he did not want meat scraps as bait. Mr. Wildlife Officer moved it a block away, this time baiting the trap with apples. The bear was caught that same night and taken up into the Flathead area. Now, wouldn't you agree this bear had exclusive tastes? Apples vs meat scraps. My green skirt vs blue jeans. It must have been a female brown bear. I mean, really, no self-respecting male bruin would be caught wearing pale green and having tart apple on its breath!

Keep up the great work, Arthur.
I feel better already!

Yours truly,
Glenness Milette & Dale Baldwin

P.S. We have painters' caps and cups from Jack Farr. We have T-shirts from Ralph Benmergui. We have Eskimo art prints from the old "Parka Patrol" program that we still miss. Yep — we're avid CBC listeners all right. How about a cup or pen or whatever from "Basic Black" for our collection? My hubby, Dale, says a book. Your book. Alright! Thanks Arthur.

February 3, 1990

Dear Arthur:

Listen to your show every week and enjoy it to the hilt! Hearing your cougar story today brings me to writing this tale. It would be back about 1978. We were sitting at our built-in booth admiring the beautiful view we never tired of, looking over Nanoose Bay. It was around 7 p.m., Sunday. Out of the blue, a beautiful cougar arrived on the lawn, sat down, lifted his leg like a house cat, cleaned his rear end, sat and had a good rest. He was so beautiful to see, as his colour was sable and coat like silk.

He ambled down our drive — the way to one neighbour's house. At that time the neighbour arrived in his sexy car and I yelled at him to hold on to Boots, his small dog, as the cougar went around his house and he could not see it from where he got out of his car. When the story got out, another neighbour heard about it and called *Victoria Sunday.* They sent up two station wagons Monday a.m. loaded with TV cameras and all their gear to get in on the action!

My husband had just arrived home off shift from 12 to 8 a.m. They asked him, where was the cougar? He had such a wonderful sense of humour. He thought, there is only one oddball on our road that would call you boys up here. "The cougar is long gone. He was here Saturday." You can imagine the hell that man gave him!

At any rate, the game warden from Nanaimo landed up with a large cage about 9 x 6 x 20, and plonked it down behind our other neighbour's house. Large enough to trap a grizzly.

The following a.m. all the neighbour found in the trap was his own cat and Boots, the tiny dog I mentioned before.

He was not the first cougar that we had a visit from. About the first snowfall we had in '75-'76, one had been at our garbage can. His tracks were so clear, I had no trouble to track his tracks in the snow; cougars' pads are just round.

Please excuse this long-winded letter. Can't explain it much better, as I don't have shorthand.

Keep up the good works and say "hello" to my cousin Bill McNeil.

All the best,
Mary (McNeil) McSweeny

Dear Arthur:

As a faithful listener of "Basic Black," I have finally found a topic on your show that I am able to make a contribution to. Today you asked the listeners to contribute their favourite wildlife stories. Well, I have a few, but there are two that really stand out. Both occurred while I was working my way through university on a work term in Northern Manitoba as a prospector. In order to have the stories make sense, you'll need a little background on this job. As prospectors we were stationed in tents in various places in the back-country of Northern Manitoba. The actual prospecting was performed using electronic instruments (not nearly as glamorous as the old pick-and-pan approach) that are carried around by crews of two along predetermined lines cut through the bush. All of this is taking place in the winter to avoid the hazards of mosquitoes and muskeg.

Back to the stories. The first occurred in the tent, in the middle of night, while I was asleep. I was awakened unceremoniously by a marauding weasel as it was foraging for food in our tent. Apparently it had decided that the fastest route from where it was to where it wanted to be was across my neck. Needless to say, I was roused with a start and, upon recognizing the culprit, immediately recalled all the images of the chickens we had had at home that were slaughtered by these feral critters. I had visions of this little monster suddenly going berserk and deciding that my neck was as good as any chicken's for a quick nip. Fortunately the weasel had no such intentions and merrily crawled along its way and made straight for my boots. At this point, I now conjured up images of being forced to suffer the use of boots *sans* laces. Well, where the thought of having my throat slashed by the flashing little teeth had frozen me, the prospect of attempting to walk on snowshoes with loose boots was enough to galvanize me to action. With a shout that woke the rest of the tent dwellers (there were four of us in the tent) I leapt from my sleeping bag to chase the intruder out. It looked at me as if I was entirely crazy and appeared to shrug as if to say "It takes all kinds . . ." and calmly sauntered out of the tent back into the great outdoors. I could almost hear it saying "Those laces couldn't have been very tasty anyway."

The second story was a little more unnerving. As I was following one of the trails in the bush, I stopped to take a reading on the instruments we used for prospecting. Taking this reading involved stopping, holding the instrument out in front of me and looking down at it until the needle on the gauge settled down, then recording the reading in the logbook that we carried. All of this took no more than a few seconds, but when I looked up to carry on down the trail, I found I was looking straight into the eyes of a large, lone wolf. This beautiful, but awesome, animal was no more than ten feet from me. We spent the next several years in the space of two seconds as we exchanged glances. Its were clearly curious, while mine were a little less composed. The impasse was broken when I blinked and the wolf took that opportunity to disappear into the bush. It was several days before I stopped looking over my shoulder for a return visit from the wolf.

There were many more interesting encounters, but few of them had the impact that these two did. Hope you keep up the good work on the radio, as your show is one of the few reasons good enough to get me out of bed on a Saturday morning. Without that prod, I'd likely forget about the day completely and sleep straight through.

Regards,
Chris Dubelaar

April 14, 1992

Dear Sir:

Sometime in early March of this year, I was listening to your program and trying to avoid work on the umpteenth essay of this semester. Needless to say, your program dealt with much more fascinating subjects than the French education system under Napoléon III (or whatever it was that I was supposed to be writing about — like much of university, it's all a blur).

That morning, you interviewed a woman by the name of Elaine Dreary who operates a *Hedgehog Hospital* in Lincolnshire, England. I was wondering if you could be so kind as to pass along her address and phone number to me.

Last summer, I was on an exchange in France. It did not take long before I noticed little piles of bones and spines scattered everywhere alongside the roadways. Despite this bounty in casualties, I did not see one live specimen in the three months I was there. My French family assures me, however, that the hedgehog is *not* extinct. I'm looking for proof.

I will be going to England next year. Please send me Ms. Dreary's address so that I might be able to finally see one of these curious little critters before it is glued flat to the pavement.

Thank you.

Yours truly,
Steven Dang

Arthur Black:

I believe I have a story (interview) idea for your show. Hope you agree. It has a spring/summer flavour, or should I say aroma.

I believe you have heard of, and possibly interviewed, New Brunswick's wetlands biologist who collects "fresh" wildlife roadkill and is compiling a roadkill cookbook.

Now, a University of New Brunswick anthropologist is asking her students — everybody — to retrieve and donate remains of wildlife so she can salvage their skeletons for teaching purposes. Salvaging can be an involved procedure.

Anthropology professor Frances Stewart says commercially prepared skeletons are becoming too expensive to purchase so she has been preparing her own. Stewart holds a variety of frozen carcasses at home; whenever she can find time — several hours — she skins, cooks, cleans and cleans and cleans the animal bones.

Do the neighbours ever complain about strange smells and backyard activities? "Rarely," says Stewart. "But I'm sure they would if they knew what I have stored on the property and what I cook outdoors. I'm not barbecuing."

So, in a quiet, manicured residential area of New Brunswick's capital city there's a bear, four bobcats and a variety of small mammals, and birds, waiting to be processed.

Frances Stewart says she needs more species and more skeletons. "Please, not too badly mauled," she adds.

CHEERS.
Stephen Branch

Dear Arthur:

I'll start out in my usual bitchy manner and complain that only on rare occasions does anybody pay any attention to the VU meter around there but it has been ever thus. In the days when I worked for that part of the contractor that carried the CBC radio feed, I was usually the one designated to keep an ear on the speakers. I always thought this was a good deal. I had the same basic complaint then as I have now. The army of technical types that my taxes go to neglect their duties more often than they perform them properly.

I don't always keep the same waking hours as my wife. I like to listen to the radio. What happens is that I am listening to something that interests me and while awaiting something else that will very likely interest me I am bombarded with loud music. Loud enough to wake the dead, let alone the light sleeper in the next room. I have registered my complaints many times to those apparently equally incompetent ones that are supposedly in charge of such things; I can confidently describe them thus because the situation doesn't seem to change.

I read your column in the local paper from where your brother resides on the neighbouring island. This brings up another pet peeve of mine: one has to reside in the land of the grey tan to work for that outfit in the position you do. I don't think there is an alternative to kicking Ontario out of Canada so that it doesn't have its way bossing the rest of the country. As for Quebec, I think they could be reasoned with. I can't say the same for the greedy manipulators in the province just to the west of them.

While I always enjoy your program, this morning's was really a gem. I wonder if I could get you to pass along my address to Matthew Saunders so that I might obtain some bat shit and the necessary plans to house it in. If we happen to leave the front door open on a summer evening they arrive in our living room. The wife lets out a yell that must not do much for the bat's nerves and heads for the bedroom and slams the door. I then herd the bat into a room with an open window. After I keep it moving for a while and it finds its way back outside. I can just imagine the conversation that the bat must have had with its mates when it got home from that night of harvesting.

I remember reading about some experiments that were being done at some institute of higher learning. Where they had a bat flying through a fan. They were trying to determine the navigating abilities of the animal. It would not hesitate to go through it until the speed was raised to 1,800 revolutions per minute. The animal seemed to know that it couldn't safely pass at any higher speed. They stated that there were no casualties from the experiment. I told the wife that there might be a job for her working around bats at some institute but she didn't seem to express much interest.

I would also appreciate receiving from Mr. Saunders a list of any publications on the subject of bats. Please don't bother sending same to the wife.

I would send you a picture for your wall but I don't have one. I even broke the camera once at the place where we get our driver's licence. They sent it to me with a statement where the picture should be stating "Valid without picture." I carried it proudly for five years. I required an ID for the phone company then. I went in to have the picture taken. I think I had the girl nearly convinced that the camera was in serious danger when I showed her my driver's pictureless licence.

Fire Chief Harry Lane

P.S. Pass on Best Regards to the techs there.

The Art of Letter Writing Is Alive and Well — Honest!

*E*ver made the blunder of putting your mouth in motion before your brain was in gear? Of course you have — that's why God gave us blushing. For most people, a verbal *faux pas* inflicts relatively limited damage — you only look stupid to the few people who overhear you. But for a radio broadcaster, well . . . let me just say I wish I had never gone on the radio and moaned about the "lost art" of letter writing.

Oh, I know we're all laserjetting into the twenty-first century. I am only too aware that it is the era of telecommunications and we have all been assigned electronic bunks in McLuhan's Global Village. But old habits die hard, and there are still an awful lot of folks out there, hiding in the underbrush along the Information Highway, staying in touch with each other the way that folks have done it since that first nameless caveman dipped his hand in red ochre and smeared it on a cave wall.

To us, it looks like gibberish. But I'll bet you a loonie to a prehistoric axehead it was the first written communication between two human beings.

It probably read: "Hi, honey, I'm off with the boys to do a little mastodon-stoning. We'll probably go out for a couple of bowls of mead. Don't wait up. Grok."

Dear Mr. Black:

I was very interested in your observation that the art of letter writing is dying, if not already dead. Somewhat unsure about what you mean by "The Art of Letter Writing," and just to show you that there is still a little life left in it, I have written you two letters — one fairly formal, and another definitely informal. You may choose the one you like the best, or enjoy the most.

As for my thoughts on the subject, I would agree that the art of letter writing is moribund, to say the least, though I would not go so far as to say it is on its last gasp and about to disappear into a welter of video clips, pornographic and violent movies, and CBC docudramas.

But let me back up a bit to ask if I may assume that you mean the actual putting down on paper various ideas your viewers may think would interest you, whether written "longhand" or typed on a typewriter or word processor. As for myself, I love to write letters. I write them to family, friends, newspaper editors, and sometimes to people I hardly know, but would like to know better. However, should you insist that I must write only formal letters to you, in cursive script, in ink on white bond paper, I fear you will be, as it is said nowadays, "out of luck."

Sometimes I like to write (type, word process) letters on brightly coloured paper. I try to choose the colour that I think the recipient will enjoy. To my delight, I find my correspondents often reply telling me how the brightly coloured paper added to the cheer of receiving my letter. Not wanting to offend your sensibilities, I shall print these letters on white fanfold paper.

Until I came to this country in 1955, the only means of communicating with my family and friends was by letter, or walk, ride my bike, or take a bus or train to where they were living and deliver my "message" by word of mouth. I used to communicate with my mother, both of us being clairvoyant, with what used to be called "vibes" — one doesn't hear the word so often today. Alas! She is no longer with us, having moved on in 1980, at the age of eighty-eight. However, even she insisted that I write to her once a month so that she could get the "chit-chat" — the not-so-important happenings and ideas. The more important happenings we flashed between us without having to put pen to paper, or lug out the typewriter.

My greatest regret has been that I can write in only two languages, English and French, though I have been known to use some Latin. In India from January 1945 to July 1947 I studied, and used to advantage, conversational Hindustani, as the language of North India was known in those days. How I wished on my return to England that I had emulated one of my heroes, Captain Sir Richard Burton, and learnt to write it, and also Urdu and Arabic. There is nothing pleases a, dare I say, "foreigner" more than to be addressed in his own language. And I am sure it must be a real delight to them to receive a letter written by another foreigner in their own language.

Do you think we should let our inability to write in another language put us off from writing? Most people, I imagine, could find a translator, but how much easier for them if they did not have to. I do know that there are some among those I count as friends who just cannot write even English sufficiently well to write a letter, and I have some family members who have an excellent education, but who just do not know how to speak to someone else in a letter. They do not reply to my letters and yet they love to receive letters themselves, and in a telephone conversation will tell me they would like me to write more often. Sometimes they will tell me that nothing interesting, or important, ever happens to them, so I ask them if, when they meet a friend on the street, or in a café, they only discuss interesting, important things.

Perhaps the art of letter writing is something like selling; one has to be a bit of a salesman, and there are precious few real salesmen about these days. I say "salesman" because in the Dale Carnegie sales course I took years ago, we had to memorize the "rules" of making a sale: Get the person's attention first, make them interested in what you are selling, convince them that what you are selling is beneficial for them. . . .

Another method of letter writing, of course, is to make use of Kipling's six little serving men — who? what? when? where? why? and how? I have found these never fail, and there is no reason whatever for their use to be confined to news stories.

Perhaps it is up to those of us who like to write letters to keep the Art (no pun intended) viable. Wouldn't you agree?

Yours sincerely,
Michael J. Bakerpearce

December 14, 1992

Dear Mr. Black:

I'm writing in response to your commentary on the lost art of letter writing. I have been aware of the demise of this wonderful habit for some time. I, for one, love to write letters and I especially enjoy receiving them.

I have one correspondent with whom I went to First Grade in public school in Toronto. She lives in Toronto and I live in Kingston — a mere 160 miles apart! However, writing has kept our friendship alive and lively for *forty-three* years. We seldom see each other but I dare say we care deeply about what happens to each other!

Perhaps modern inventions have led to the demise of the handwritten letter. Who knows? It is very sad. For there is nothing stirs my heart more than to gather up my mail and find a missive from my girlhood friend. It's sad that more people don't value this simple, warm sign of caring.

I know one must take care in what one writes — because once it's gone, it's gone! However, if I ever write anything I'm doubtful about I always keep it for a day and think it over.

I have acquired two more pen pals. One in California who exchanges recipes with me and one in Victoria, B.C. We haven't met. With one correspondent in particular I have formed a bond and I look forward to her lavender envelopes! (We also exchange poetry.)

My children always wondered why I got so many letters! And they didn't get any! I explained: in order to receive letters you must write letters — and even then there's no guarantee people will reply!

Sincerely,
(Mrs.) June Holloway

Dear Mr. Black:

We enjoy your comments each Friday evening. They brighten the "gloom and doom" of the newscasts.

But this Friday you threw out a challenge: "Write to me, and I'll write to you."

I write letters, at least two a week to family and overseas, and never miss, and enjoy the time I spend putting pen to paper. To me, it's as near to a "chat" as I can get.

Since way back in 1936, when I married, and left England's shores for Shanghai, China, I wrote my mother each week and they went "via Siberia" at that time. A move to Australia in 1941 until my return to England in 1946; the letters went on.

In October of 1951 another move, to Canada, and my weekly letters to my family, and my mother, carried on until she passed away in 1958. Then weekly epistles went on to my brother, and since he passed away in 1980, the letters still go each week to my sister.

Of course I write to others in between and recently mailed fifteen letters and cards to old friends and family in Ireland, Scotland and England.

Now, in my seventy-ninth year, my fingers are a little crooked and maybe a word is spelled wrongly, but I know those to whom I write will overlook that.

Now Mr. Black, keep up your witty comments; there's many like myself get a real chuckle.

Sincerely,
Joan Fischer

December 16, 1992

Hi Arthur!

No doubt about it — letters are a breath of fresh air!

And I couldn't know it better than when I was at the University of Guelph in the early '70s. First time away from home, I wrote, and my friends and family wrote back. Regularly. Incredible therapy for the homesick.

Then there was Lakehead U. in T. Bay! Yes, I was there in '79–'81. You were on the radio noon show in C.B.Q. The good ol' days. You interviewed me once also, when I was on contract with the M.N.R. in Kenora. I was looking for information from naturalists who might have visited certain provincial parks on my study list.

Those days I wrote and received from family and especially friends. What a great feeling to see letters in the box after walking home in an early November blizzard in Kenora.

Then I was in Saudi Arabia in '84–'85. Two years in an incredibly new culture. And boy, did I *need* letters there. Got them too. Still have them *all*! What a collection of history, and a very special life diary in a way.

I still get letters from special friends. And if they can't write for whatever reason, I know they think of me.

Yes, the feeling of an empty mailbox can be excruciatingly lonely, especially when you really need that hello. Even if it's only a short note, or card.

It's never too late to write. There's never "not enough time." It only takes a few minutes to jot a few lines. To hell with computers, fax machines, etc. A pen and paper are the best for therapy. The price of a stamp is no excuse. A coffee's just the same. Usually more!!

So Arthur, here's to you, and me, and letters! I thoroughly enjoyed you while in Northern Ontario. Actually met you once too, at a Christmas drive in Victoriaville Mall in F.W.

By the way, I got my degree at L.U., and now own and operate the business on this letterhead (landscaping). But I miss the North. Don't we all?

Cheers, Arthur. All the best! (Eh!?)

Allan Goddard

June 14, 1992

Dear Arthur (if I may; "Mr. Black" seems wrong somehow):

Many thanks for your gracious and ultra-generous comments Saturday about "G's Albums" and my eightieth birthday.

Such a tribute on your famous program means a lot to a fellow-broadcaster. I don't go in much for publicity, but an occasional on-the-air assessment by another inhabitant of the same network is something to appreciate.

Barbara and I also enjoyed your lively basement chat with that amazing gent David Lennick. He seems so young (especially to an "octo"), but his mental computer's info banks go back to the primitive beginnings of recorded sound. Maybe Lennick is a helluva lot older than he looks. His face — or a clone of it — can be seen among the Union soldiers in *several* of Matthew Brady's photos of the Civil War.

By the way, Barbara thinks you do my "Hello!" better than I do. In case I completely lose the hang of it, maybe you'll consider putting your version on a tape cartridge that I could hold in reserve, ready for emergencies in Studio K.

Thanks again, cheers, and all the best.

Clyde Gilmour

Dear Arthur:

I want to assure you I'm *not* trying to enmesh you in a marathon chain of correspondence. This happened a few years ago when Barbara's answer to a listener's letter from Winnipeg so tickled him that he wrote back thanking her for replying. *That* letter was so gracious that Barbara wrote again, thanking him for his thank-you. And so it went, back and forth at least seven times before one or other of them, probably Mr. Winnipeg, bellowed, "*Enough*, already!"

The fact is, nonetheless, that I thanked you for your generous sign-off tribute to my old show and to my new awesome status as an OCTO. Then you thanked Barbara and me with one of your cheery cards. Now I find myself absolutely obligated to tell you that the mailbag arising from "Basic Black" just never stops. I feel nerdish writing again so soon, but on the other hand I'd feel churlish — much worse than nerdish — if I neglected to drop you a further note. But not even Miss Manners herself would rebuke you if "Enough, already!" were *your* sensible response.

Cheers,
Clyde Gilmour

*This Train's Got,
the Disappearin'
Railroad Blues*

—Steve Goodman song lyric

*W*e all do, Steve. Of all the bodychecks poor old Canada took in the last couple of decades, none was more poignant than the loss of our passenger trains. It was trains that first hemstitched this country together. Trains carried our pioneers west, and later they carried farm boys dressed in khaki back east to sail across the Atlantic.

They are fading from the fabric of this country now, like a train whistle in the night. Abandoned lines are being torn up and the "railway cuts" that used to glisten with twin steel snakes for as far as the eye could see are returning to burdock, chicory and dogwood. Towns that used to hum with life from the sawtoothed Rockies to the balding hills of Newfoundland have dried up, sagged, and vanished from the map.

I once met a conductor on a train going through Sioux Lookout. He said if he was prime minister, the first thing he'd do is give every Canadian teenager a free transCanada rail pass, so that they could all, just once, see the depth and breadth of this magnificent country from the window of a train.

He would have had my vote. Now it's too late.

They're pretty well gone, the passenger trains.

Gone, but not forgotten.

Dear Arthur:

It must be at least fifty years since I took this memorable train trip but it still raises a chuckle whenever I happen to think about it again.

At that time I was teaching in Hedley, a small gold-mining town in B.C. The Kettle Valley line of the CPR had been completed some years previously linking towns and communities from the Rockies to Vancouver.

I was planning a trip to Vancouver for a few days and so was a friend of mine. We agreed to meet in Penticton and travel together.

The train left Penticton at about eleven o'clock at night and arrived in Vancouver about seven the next morning. Rather than sitting up all night as we usually did, we decided to splurge and share the expense of a sleeper.

The sleeping car was a normal coach during the day but at night the porter made up the berths — the lower one by sliding the two facing seats together to form a bed, and the upper by lowering a curved overhead shelf which was fixed to the wall above the window and fastened to the ceiling above. When this was lowered it formed a bed above the lower berth. In order to provide privacy, partitions were slid into position between the berths. Green curtains were hung from the upper and lower berths on the side facing the corridor. A small ladder was attached to one side to provide access to the upper berth.

By the time the train arrived in Penticton the porter had made up all the berths and all the passengers had retired for the night. We had opted for a lower berth. There wasn't much room to spare so I trotted off to the washroom to freshen up while Jill changed into her pyjamas. When I returned she trotted off to the washroom and I undressed and settled down for the night.

After a few minutes I heard a whisper: "Psst! Psst! Is that you, Marian?"

"Yes," I replied. And with that Jill scrambled in beside me and began to giggle.

"What's so funny?" I asked.

When she settled down she told me. She had returned along the corridor and hopped into the berth she was sure was ours. Thinking that I was the recumbent figure curled up near the window she said, "Marian, let's sleep spoon fashion. There'll be more room that way."

There was a pause, and then a voice (definitely a masculine one) spoke up. "That's just fine with me, ma'am, but I'm not Marian."

With that, Jill leapt out of the bed, apologizing profusely. Anxious not to repeat the performance she decided to check out the next berth first. As it happened it was ours!

Naturally we were curious and intrigued. Who was the man Jill had so unceremoniously surprised? Was he young or old, handsome or plain, interesting or ordinary?

When we arose next morning we noticed that most of the berths had been taken apart and returned to day use and the passengers had gone for breakfast or departed as the train was in the station.

When we entered the dining car we scanned the tables. Was the man who had had an unexpected visitor last night having breakfast? Would he suspect one of us?

As we sat down at our table we noticed across the corridor and down one table a lone man — yes, he was young and good looking and probably interesting too — busily eating his bacon and eggs. Without looking up he lifted up one spoon, put it down and nestled another inside it!

Sincerely,
Marian Robertson

Dear Arthur:

I am a CP Rail pensioner now, but in the late 1940s and '50s was involved in the movement of refugees (displaced persons) coming to Canada through the ports of Halifax and Saint John.

These people had been through difficult times and luxury items had not appeared in their rations for many years. Ice cream was only a memory to the adults and unknown to the children.

The first meal on the Canadian train was usually the evening meal and consisted of a thick soup, roast beef with vegetables, ice cream and coffee or milk.

Our waiters soon realized ice cream was a real treat to the children and on their own arranged a little presentation.

After the roast beef was finished the plates would be removed and the waiters would line up in the pantry to load their trays with ice cream. Then, trays held high, they would enter the dining car and serve only the children.

The children would look at the square of white cold stuff and then look up at their parents to find out if they should eat it. The parents would smile and nod. The children would take a bit, taste the flavour and then a smile of utter pleasure would come over their faces.

By this time the waiters would have obtained more servings of ice cream and started serving the adults, with second help-ings going to the children.

I still remember the expressions on the faces of children eating vanilla ice cream for the first time.

Hugh McMillan

Dearest Art:

My most memorable train experience?

Well, it wasn't exactly a train, it was one of those little motor-cars, called speeders; but I wasn't *on* it . . . in fact no one was!

I'd better explain . . .

I once lived, in the foggy ruins of time, in a tipi quite near the BC Rail line between Pemberton and D'Arcy, B.C.

A speeder used to follow every freight by about half an hour in the summer to watch for fires that the "heavy" may have set . . .

I used to wave to the guy who was the firewatch, whenever I was at home, and he would wave back, *de rigueur*, except for one sunny Saturday morning when I emerged from the blissful comfort of the tipi to yawn and stretch and mosey over to the woodpile and prepare for breakfast eventually, when I heard the ol' firewatch blistering along, as per usual, some distance up the trax and through the sweetly scented firs, out of my line of sight; leaving the woodpile I manoeuvred myself to a small clearing so we could have our "Wave," as brief as this one sounded like it was going to be, judging by the speed he was going . . . sometimes this guy was in a hurry . . . and then go on about our respective business . . . So I stand there, waiting, waving, through the little break in the trees where I knew he would look for me, when to my utter horror the thing went roaring past, fairly normal, but with no operator! And full tilt! (My wave at this point must have lost some of its animated enthusiasm.)

Not having a phone, obviously (although BC Tel had offered to install one for me . . . in the tipi . . . I could just hear it . . . RIINNNGGG . . .) I ran the mile or so to the neighbour's to use *his* . . . I knew the Budd car was due to be heading south in about twenty-five minutes at that spot, so wanted to try to give the good men on *that* piece of equipment a bit of a warning . . . I phoned the Pemberton station and frantically explained the situation to the somewhat sleepy, somewhat unresponsive, to me, BC Rail employee . . . he seemed to take minutes to realize that he had to get on the radio to the Budd, and I was beside myself when he said, "They're not answering . . . I'll try it again in a couple of minutes . . ."

. . . I walked home, all ears, expecting at any second to hear a minor, or so, explosion or crash or *commotion* somewhere down the valley, all the time on tiptoes, just praying that no one got hurt, when WHO should I meet coming up the tracks in the opposite direction but the firewatch *himself*, on foot, with a very red face and a very large armful of the most wonderful wildflowers, which he had occasion to pick, he explained, in a lull in his duties, miles back down the wild line, and illustrated for me, from behind the large profuse bouquet, and quite out of breath, how when he was nimbly leaping on to the suddenly-GOING speeder (which apparently had to be jump-started, throttle full-ON), with his flowers — "Lovely, aren't they?" — his foot slipped, and rather than chuck the glorious harvest of colour and scent, he had chosen instead, in the split second which he *had*, to let the finicky *speeder* go . . . the result of which was my rudely ruined calmness, not to mention breakfast . . .

As we stood there, him with his flowers and me in an absolute tizzy about an imminent crash, the Budd whistle suddenly droned out watchfully from the crossing a half-mile north, and the firewatch and I could only just amble off the trax and wait, speechless, and sniff the flowers . . .

And sure enough along comes old reliable and her happy crew, none the worse for wear, but for one slightly nasty dent in her stainless cowling, all smiles . . . (turns out those speed-

ers are designed to separate quite harmlessly on impact . . .
but apparently *not so* for firewatchmen, as he kept his job, on
a new speeder, just as happy-go-lucky as ever) . . . We had
coffee and hotcakes together, by a lazy fire, with the big splen-
dorous bouquet in a large pail of creekwater in the tipi while
we ate, and laughed . . .

Yours, still rather in awe, truly,
Al Lewis

Dear Arser:

I may call you Arser, mayn't I? Twaddle, poppycock and tommyrot. That's what your show is. I try to listen to it every week.

The train memory. I grew up at Seebe, Alberta, about fifty miles west of Calgary on the CPR main line. In 1960 I was 8, and I woke up in the middle of the night from hearing a prolonged loud crash, then went back to sleep. In the morning, I looked out the window toward the tracks, and there were boxcars tumbled over and piled up like a bunch of puppies sleeping next to their mother. I had to rush out and see it all. So did all the other kids in town. The one-room school was empty that morning. They got the main line running and open by about midnight, but the cleanup went on for over a week. Grain and newsprint were piled all over. The work train with its crane piling the broken boxcars was fascinating to watch. The section gang, who all spoke with broken English — "Whata you-a wanto? Goway." — were something incomprehensible to us.

After the cleanup was done, my dad gave me a bunch of gunny sacks and a coal scuttle and told me he would pay me 25¢ for each sack of grain I could clean up off the ground. I made four dollars and a quarter. Our chickens ate well for a long time. For about the next five years, I got up every morning and looked out the window for another train wreck. Excitement and money, but it never happened again.

Goodbye Arser.
Colin Reid

March 3, 1990

Dear Sir:

In February, 1931, I arrived in Canada at age 18. Young people from Great Britain and western Europe were sponsored by a government program. In return for our passage, we undertook to work as domestics or farm-labourers for a minimum of 12 months.

Disembarking in Halifax, N.S., we were put on a train for Montreal. Severe ladies dressed in Hudson seal coats kept an eye on us. In a town in New Brunswick, we heard that the train would be stopping for a while. A group of us decided to get off and walk around a bit.

One of the girls fell in the snow and became hysterical, thinking her hands would freeze. We decided that we would go into a nearby restaurant, so that she could recover.

Imagine our horror, on coming out of the restaurant, to see the train callously chugging its way out of the valley, with all our belongings.

All turned out well. We waited 10–12 hours for the next train, but we were in no hurry. I had acquired a shipboard sweetheart who was along with us.

On arrival in Montreal, the ladies in seal coats greeted us with disdain and we were put on trains for our eventual destination. Mine was Kingston, Ontario, so I said goodbye to my shipmates who were going in a different direction.

I found a job right away, and, as they say, have never "looked back" since.

Anne Kuntz

Dear Arthur:

I'm bogged down with stuff to write but your piece in this week's *Tribune* prompts me to sound off to you.

A couple of months ago a fellow passenger on the train was a railway engineer. He was going to Toronto to pick up his train which I believe was going north. Anyhow, he worked four days then had seven days off. It worked out to about twenty hours a week and he had already earned over $50,000. He would have more than $60,000 by the end of December — and no overtime.

Now to backtrack. When I published a newspaper in Pictou, N.S., a Halifax train-buff club chartered a train for a trip to Pictou. Every ticket was sold and I believe there were seven or eight coaches. The trip was 100 miles there and 100 miles back. Even though all the tickets were sold in advance, the train carried a full crew, including I seem to recall four conductors plus the engineer and fireman and the rest of the crew. That was not all. According to union regulations, they had to change crews at Truro, a division point. All the crew, engineers, brakemen, firemen, conductors . . . Then when they got to New Glasgow, another division point, they had to change crews again. This third crew took the train to Pictou, eight miles, waited an hour or so and took it back to New Glasgow. A fourth crew took the train to Truro, and a fifth crew back to Halifax.

The trip was twelve hours. Five full crews all paid a day's wages. I forget the precise figures but the wages alone were about ten times the total revenue with all tickets sold. My article was picked up by some rail official and I received a letter from the head of CN public relations who thanked me and said the article had been copied and circulated to their senior staff.

That is only part of the problem. You and I and everyone else who buys petrol help to pay for highways that are used by eighteen-wheel trucks hauling thirty or forty tons. The railways, on the other hand, not only must build and maintain their roadways, they must also pay property taxes on their real-estate roadways.

I could go on at some length but I'm inclined to agree with the AMTRAK manager who spoke at Saint John a few weeks ago. He said better to let VIA strangle itself to death and start over again.

Enjoy catching your Saturday morning program but pick up only part of it when I'm going to market or some such.

Cheers,
George Cadogan

Dear Arthur:

This is a note of encouragement and congratulations on your radio essay of January 20 about the cancellation of the VIA train on which you travelled between Guelph and Toronto. You were brave to speak out. I hope they don't cancel your show! I share your feelings exactly. The train from Kingston to Toronto which used to pass through Port Hope was also axed. I have been using that train for twenty-two years.

You may remember me. I was on your show last June. I am the author of a book called *Pomp and Circumstances*. Quite apart from having been a guest myself, I do enjoy your show very much. Keep up the good work. And keep on harassing the government to restore passenger train service within the conurbation of Toronto. I don't think the current government knows just how many of us are fuming mad and greatly inconvenienced.

Yours truly,
Claire Mowat

January 20, 1990

Dear Arthur:

Bravo for your comments on VIA Rail cuts, broadcast this morning. Your comments are usually fun and cogent. Today they were right on. I particularly valued your observation about breaking an election pledge by the Conservative government. You might recall they broke a similar undertaking after their first election, when they attempted to de-index old-age pensions. Perhaps if citizens squawk loud and long enough, the VIA cutbacks can be rolled back, too. I would commend to your attention that in the mid-seventies the Liberals began the process of dismantling rail passenger travel when they introduced VIA. I recall hearing on the radio David Lewis making the point that the Liberals were permitting the CPR to abrogate their contract to provide passenger rail traffic *in perpetuity* in return for other considerations, e.g., many vast real-estate holdings, timber, mineral rights, etc. If the CPR wanted to give up one part of their contract, the government was in a position to insist that they give up other parts, too.

The Liberals declined to do this.

At the same time, the Tories clamoured that the process used by the Liberals was tainted. That is, VIA was introduced by the Trudeau Liberals by order-in-council, short-circuiting the democratic forum of Parliament. Some of the Tories pursued the issue of process through the courts, which ruled that under the legislation, it was legal to introduce the sweeping legislation of creating VIA Rail to perform the passenger service duties of the CPR and CNR by means of order-in-council

(Cabinet decree) rather than through the House of Commons. Hear any complaint from the Tories or Liberals about subverting democratic process this time around?

Keep up the good work.

In appreciation,
Berrel Garshowitz

Dear Arthur:

I guess I've gone across this country by train five times. That leaves me out here as all my flights have been round trips. The first was fulfilling my East Coast girl's dream. Head west young woman, seek adventure and romance. February of 1975, I was eighteen. Just left home and travelling with my brother and his girl friend. That train, it carried me, it took me, showing off the huge wild beauty between where you'd been and where you'd be. Lake Superior, it seems like it hung on longer than just one day. Then I'd keep finding out it was still Ontario. It was being kind of a hog. As the country was going to be five days long, seems it consumed about three.

The Prairies having to be so endless to convince you they weren't a dream. Only the train it seems can stop you like that, maybe the middle of the night and show you that empty street, that sleeping town. Imagining your life there; the way you dream you have a horse and would ride through, your long wild hair matching the mane of your beast. You'd stop there in the middle of the town that stopped the train, and you'd dare there to be a cowboy man enough to jump off . . . I'm sure there is also a practical side to riding the train. And I hope I never see that fantasy on a beer commercial . . .

Seems you started into the Rockies in time to have them most of the day and night hide their ending. I rode the CN and the CP. Seems you caught the Fraser River going back east in the fall. You knew you were back east when the trees got small and slim, and the woods let you walk right through. You know you are out west in B.C. when it's like an impenetrable rain forest and the ground hides under that tripping tangle of salal.

You could fly around in circles blindfolded and somehow tell by the smell and feel of the salt air whether it is Atlantic or Pacific.

In one of those coaches I met "Champagne Charlie" and he played train rambling songs I'd never heard. The island in the middle of the big windy Winnipeg street. Someone knew where to get the best fries in the country, that there was enough time. Was it in Edmonton you could make it to the Y for a shower?

Did they unite in '79? That was my last round trip. It was with my husband and two kids then two years old and eight months old. We had our box of food under the seat of our "section" which was two upright seats in the day, two bunks at night. It was an old car, the heating system had had it. The porter showed Billy how to shut it down when it threatened to cook its occupants. Then the car would get progressively colder. It was December. The pride that was CN's or CP's was lost in VIA Rail. I'd thought the kids would sleep lots, be lulled to sleep by the motion. Eight-month-old Melisse wanted to do the backbreaking two-thumb-grip walk. You couldn't just let her cry about not getting to.

When I walked through the Third Class cars it looked like the Depression had hit. I guess they probably got some new pride in VIA. Oh, and there was the dome car. I want to ride across again. Get off wherever I want. Now there's haunted empty stations? So many cannot leave home by train or go home by train. Break the country's heart.

Most sincerely yours,
Renée McKee

Dear Arthur:

Re: My Love Affair with Passenger Trains

I listen to you every Saturday morning and feel as if I know you personally. Maybe someday I will have the pleasure of meeting you in person.

I am originally from Saskatchewan, born here and grew up and went to school here in Regina. I lived in Toronto for thirty-one years, having married a Toronto man. My four children and two grandchildren live in and around Toronto.

Now for my tale of my:

Love for Passenger Trains

I was only eighteen years of age and I was travelling via the Dominion passenger train from Regina to British Columbia for my annual vacation. My twin sister was with me. We boarded the train at night and after being settled in our berths we decided to explore some of the other cars. We discovered the dinette car, dining lounge and eventually the dome car. We were sitting there enjoying the scenery of the trip when a couple of men sitting behind us tried to strike up a conversation. It was a two-day trip to the coast and they wanted to play cribbage with us to pass the time. One was an older married Army man and the other was a single younger Navy man returning to British Columbia from his annual leave in Toronto. He was stationed in Esquimalt. To make a long story short this man became my future husband and we have been married over thirty-one years. I came home from that holiday with an engagement ring on my left hand. Eight months later we were married.

The really amazing part of the story is that in August 1957, when we met, there were two passenger trains from Toronto to B.C.: the Dominion, which stopped at every whistle-stop along the CP route, and the Canadian, which followed the CN northern route and was an express passenger train, only stopping at the bigger cities, and would have gone to Saskatoon instead of Regina. For some uncanny reason my husband was unable to get a ticket for the faster train. If that had happened we would never have met.

MY ETERNAL THANKS TO CP RAIL.

Sincerely yours,
(Mrs.) Jean Woods

Get Plastered, and Call Me in the Morning

"Basic Black"'s resident sawbones, Doctor Ted Boadway, would probably never agree with me, but there's a lot to be said for good old homegrown, over-the-garden-fence cure-alls.

I can hear Ted as he reads this. He's making noises like a duck: quack, quack, quack . . .

But I remember my grandma Gilder. She lived an incredibly hard life in the dirt-poor backwoods of Ontario, acting as a midwife and raising two young daughters on her own. But she was tougher than anything life could throw at her. I have a vision of her out in the vegetable garden in a long black dress, still pulling weeds and thinning vegetables well into her late eighties.

She wasn't one to complain, but she always wore a copper bracelet. For her rheumatism.

Don't get me wrong, Grandma was no superstitious old biddy. She hated that copper bracelet. She thought it was gaudy. Besides, it made her arm green.

And she knew her doctor laughed at her for wearing it.

Only thing was . . . when she wore it, her rheumatism went away.

Grandma Gilder also swore by mustard plasters. Now, how many thousand schoolkids do you reckon you'd have to interrogate before you found one who knew what a mustard plaster was? They're even more defunct than our passenger trains.

There was a time, however, when the mustard plaster was prescribed for just about anything that ailed you.

And a lot of "Basic Black" listeners remember those days.

Dear Arthur:

I must begin by telling you how much I enjoy your program "Basic Black," which I pick up on Saturday mornings from CBC North, in Sudbury. After a hectic week and just before I launch out into preparations for Sunday, I find it very relaxing and, in most cases, quite thought provoking.

Earlier this morning I was interested in your conversation with a Doctor Ted Something-or-other (sorry, I missed his surname) about the old-fashioned mustard plaster. Boy, did that bring back memories! I hesitate to contradict or try to correct a medical doctor, but my memories and understanding of that old-fashioned remedy are somewhat different than his. All that may mean of course is that I am so much older than he, to paraphrase an old song.

In the days of the Great Depression most families were hard pressed to pay a doctor's fee for a house call, even though doctors were so notoriously generous when they knew their patients were so short of money. That being the case, the "home remedy" was more often than not the old standby. When anyone in our family had a very bad chest cold, dear Mother would always appear at the bedroom door with all the "fixins" for that tried and true remedy. Instead of grinding up mustard seeds, our mother always used the dried mustard which came in a can. The same brand is still available today in most stores but I will not mention the name as we must not give free advertising. It still sits in my kitchen cupboard in its large yellow tin. Once this was mixed into a rather thick paste by adding just the exact amount of water it was then spread on a piece of brown paper. The best type of paper to use was the kind the local butcher used to wrap the meat he delivered to your door. This paper was always cleaned very thoroughly when the meat was unwrapped and saved for such situations. Remember, these were Depression days, and you even saved the string which was used to tie up the package! The mustard plaster was then placed upon your chest with the paper between the paste and your skin. This was to prevent severe burning. The whole thing was usually covered by a piece of flannelette, double thickness if it was large enough, and your pyjama coat was buttoned up over it and the bed covers pulled up over you again. Did it work? Your doctor is obviously a Doubting Thomas, but not so with doctors of my childhood years. They almost always prescribed it for severe chest colds being treated at home. And yes, it did work! You may still doubt the value and the efficacy of such a remedy, but I and many, many more folks of years gone by will swear by all that is holy that the hot, smelly mustard plaster does work. If they do not work today it is probably because most people do not know how to make them properly or how to administer them.

To the horror and sometimes great amusement of a number of my friends in the medical profession I have mentioned such other remedies as sulphur and molasses; hot goose grease and camphorated oil; and the tried and true Indian remedy of hot spruce tea brewed from a "medicine bird" made of tender spruce twigs. By the way, two of those spruce twig "medicine birds" sit on the top of my stereo in my living room here in Timmins. When one discovers how many of our prescription drugs today are based on the old-fashioned remedies known to the native "medicine man" and gathered from the Canadian woods or the jungles of South America, one learns very quickly not to despise those home remedies of long ago or to suggest that any belief in their efficacy was due to nothing more than a mild case of superstition.

The next time you have a cold, Arthur, don't take two aspirin and go to bed intending to call your doctor in the morning. Just look up an old-fashioned remedy book, and follow the instructions carefully using some common sense and discretion, and you will save yourself a lot of money on prescription drugs, and take a heavy burden off our Medicare system. You will also be pleasantly surprised by the results! "Eh, what's up, Doc?"

Sincerely,
Richard S. Mowry, T.O.S.

February 14, 1990

Dear Mr. Malahoss:

First let me say that CBC is my favourite station — especially Saturdays and Sundays. So last Saturday, February 10 — while listening to "Basic Black" — Arthur announced that he was having a doctor to comment on the pros and cons of the mustard plaster. I expected to hear some intelligent information coming from an educated professional man. I know the great strides that have been made in medicine but there are some old-fashioned cures that don't have to be written off. Perhaps they're not as easy as taking chemicals into our bodies but if they work why knock it? This Dr. Ted (Boldwen?) didn't do his homework. He admitted he had never tried it. Said that the mustard had to be black. (Did you ever hear of black mustard?) "MP didn't have any purpose except to blister the skin and promote mustard sales," according to him. He doesn't have a clue how to apply it. The chest has to be rubbed with vaseline first. The poultice is made with 1 tbsp. mustard to three parts flour and enough water to be made into a med. paste on a J cloth or cheese cloth, put on chest and covered with plastic to keep moisture in and left on for 15–20 minutes or until skin is pink. It's a nice warm feeling, penetrating deeply and loosening the problem or congestion. During World War I there was a serious epidemic of influenza in Winnipeg. Many people died. My mother claimed that she saved my father (who had double pneumonia) with mustard plasters. Later whenever anyone in the family had congestions she treated us the same way.

104

When I had children and my son got pneumonia an excellent baby specialist was recommended (Dr. Shapiro). He prescribed a medication and mild mustard plasters.

Then when my grandchildren were sick and staying with me (after some coaxing) they let me give them the treatment and had to admit it was comforting and helpful. Now they have named it "Grandma's Voodoo Cure" — but grandma is a "good witch," and it does work.

Thank you for letting me say this.

Sincerely,
(Mrs.) Ollie Hillman

P.S. Now I must give myself a mustard plaster. Feel a cough coming on.

Dear Sirs:

I heard your program yesterday, February 10, and thought I should write you before some innocent soul took your advice re mustard plasters. You didn't mention flour in your recipe. Just mustard and water. I believe I owe my life to the judicious use of mustard plasters when I was a child. But the mixture we used was two parts of flour, one part mustard and water. Your mix would cause blistering. If you don't believe me, just try it out on yourself.

Yours,
M. A. Gould

February 10, 1990

Dear Mr. A. Black:

I am writing about your *Black Magic* book. I have a story that I hope will grant me a book. I am seventy-two years old, and the eldest of twelve children, six boys and six girls; this story goes back to January and February 1942.

My mother had a heart condition. She couldn't speak, I had to be her mouth speech. Doctor's orders. He ordered mustard plasters every twenty minutes, to be put on my mother's chest; it was terrible mixing that so often, and looking after all those kids.

My dad just managed to keep bread on the table, so we couldn't afford help. They are both gone now. My mother died February 1942 and the first thing I noticed on the floor in the doorway of her room was the mustard plaster where she had thrown it. I am a believer in old remedies. The doctor of that time gave the mustard plaster a wonderful name. I enjoy and listen to CBC every morning and evening, so hoping to hear from you in due course. I thank you.

Sincerely,
Mrs. Mary Collins

February 10, 1990

Dear Arthur Black:

I have just been listening to your discussion about mustard plasters, and would like to add a few words to it, in their favour.

A number of years ago, in the mid-'50s, and just before the accepted use of antibiotics for many health problems (few on the market, and so few used), it became necessary for me to nurse both my parents at home — one with viral pneumonia, the other with lobar pneumonia. The hospital plan had just begun in Saskatchewan, and beds were not available.

As a young woman, with no nursing experience at all, and few medications to choose from, I soon became an expert at the Art of Mustard Plasters!! I used good-old-fashioned dry mustard, kitchen-type, flour and water, held together with cheese cloth and brown paper. The proportions used escape me, but the end results were miraculous! Although I know it is not feasible to believe that a substance applied to the skin can help congestion in the lungs, nevertheless it did!

In those days, pneumonia patients were often almost written off, so it was indeed a victory we won.

I often thought about the above, while nursing my own three children through a number of situations. The prescribed medications were indeed efficacious, time-saving, and easily taken, but at who knows just what cost, and I was always grateful that such medicines were rarely needed.

Your program is a regular and important part of our Saturdays. Many thanks!!

Yours very truly,
Barbara Butler

February 12, 1990

Dear Arthur:

Listening to you and your Dr. guest scoff at the merits of mustard plasters Saturday a.m., Feb. 10, I just had to write to tell you that mustard plasters do break heavy chest colds. I am over seventy years old and have used them all my life on myself and my family. The recipe is one part dry mustard, two parts flour, one tsp. baking soda mixed with warm water to thick paste. Spread on cloth, large enough to cover chest, place another cloth over plaster and place on chest. If cold is very heavy put one on the back too.

The baking soda prevents the plaster from blistering. Leave plaster on patient till skin is pink. Remove plaster. May be repeated after four hours. An absolute must. Patient must spend the next day in bed.

Before the days of antibiotics I can assure you that mustard plasters played a major role in curing a lot of colds.

"Basic Black" Listener,
Mary Waldbauer

The Greening of "Basic Black"

a few years ago, while lingering over coffee in a restaurant on Saltspring Island, I noticed a potted plant. Each leaf on the plant had hundreds and hundreds of tiny seedlings dangling off its edges. It looked like a kind of botanical surrey with a fringe on top. The waiter told me it was a Mexican Hat plant. On impulse, I slipped a few seedlings into a CBC envelope, promptly forgot all about it, and flew back to Toronto.

Several weeks later, while cleaning out my backpack, I came upon the wrinkled envelope. I opened it. A few wizened husks of seedlings rattled on to my desk. Dead as a doornail, undoubtedly. And yet . . . on another impulse I picked up the least moribund-looking one, pinched some dirt out of one of Gzowski's geraniums, and planted the seedling in a styrofoam coffee cup.

Two days later it was half an inch high. Two months later it was growing in its own pot and clawing at the acoustic tiles in my office ceiling. Each leaf was also sporting its own fringe of seedlings. Nothing could stop my Black Beauty.

Except perhaps the CBC.

About this time all employees got a memo "discouraging" them from taking any plants to the new CBC headquarters we were moving to.

They didn't want to have any — you know — "foreign contaminants" interfering with the technological purity of the new Broadcast Centre.

I know a threat of genocide when I hear it. Instantly I alerted "Basic Black" listeners to my dilemma. Naively, I asked if anyone out there would like one of Black Beauty's seedlings . . . .

December 12, 1992

Dear "Basic Black" Correspondence Handler:

I have never written to your program before. In fact, I have never written to any other program or medium to express an opinion about that medium or the world in general. The only reason I choose to foray into correspondence with your program now is that I heard the host of your program, Mr. Arthur Black, announce that he was giving away seeds of a plant to any that cared to write in for them. Now, I understand that this plant is a very dear one to Mr. Black. Being myself a long-time fan of his program, I recognized that this was finally the time to write my inaugural letter to a major medium, so that I could perhaps be a little bit closer to Mr. Black with my very own offspring of his plant.

Please, Mr./Ms. Handler, could I have a seed of my very own? And could I possibly have another three for three of my family who have been fans for longer than me? (We all live separately, I promise.) If you could do this for me, I won't ever bother you with another letter, I promise. And, I could have a very economical Christmas.

Thank you very much.

Sincerely,
Christopher Whitehead

December 14, 1992

Dear Arthur:

I have never in my life sent a letter to CBC Radio. But while listening to your program my heartstrings were tugged and then practically yanked from me. Hence, with PC at my fingertips I am sending this to you.

Being a plant lover, I find it terribly sterile that CBC will not allow their employees to take their precious oxygen-giving friends along to the new domain. However, the poor plants would probably die in that dark, breathless environment. Therefore, I would love to open my home to any or many of your Mexican Hat's little sombreros.

Good luck to you in your sunless, climatized tomb. Maybe you should run away with your little sombreros to a sunny, airy location.

Sincerely,
Denise J. Galloway

P.S. Have a very Merry Christmas! I thoroughly enjoy your show.

December 12, 1992

Dear Arthur:

My heart goes out to you. I can visualize that new Broadcasting Centre because I used to work in a building just like it. It and the inhabitants who were happy there seemed so soulless that eventually I quit. I'm now a freelance writer eking out a rather precarious existence from an office in my tiny upstairs back bedroom. But it does have a window that opens, a view of the bird feeders for when the words aren't flowing well, and a radio I can listen to freely without headphones when I'm printing or proofreading. And the household cat reminds me that despite her best efforts we probably still have one cunning mouse living in the wall.

I would consider it a real honour to provide a home for an offspring of Black Beauty — if you have one left. I promise I will treat it with the mixture of love and neglect that has always worked splendidly for my crop of thriving Christmas cacti, pothos, and philodrendrons.

Good luck, in your new "home" — and, as always, thanks for a wonderful show.

Cheers,
Paddy Muir

Dear Arthur:

I am shocked and outraged. I can't believe that a world-class information service is so backward as to allow a sealed climate-controlled environment in the new broadcast building. The '50s are over and so are the '60s, '70s and '80s for that matter.

With "Ideas," "Quirks and Quarks," "As It Happens," "Witness," and countless news and current-event programs, has anybody at CBC ever learned anything about life on the third planet out in this solar system?

It works like this. Walking, talking, sneezing, coughing, urinating, excreting, completely mobile bipeds sometimes found in a humanoid form are busy moving in and out of buildings carrying all kinds of disease while constantly exhaling a gas which to themselves is poisonous.

At the same time there are, thank God, other lifeforms on this planet that make it their business to take this poisonous gas and convert it to life-giving oxygen on which these bipeds depend for their very survival. Wake up!!!!

I have a computer store in Sydney and am proud to co-inhabit this high-tech environment with a family of Dieffenbachias that not only refresh the air in this joint constantly but bring constant joy to my patrons as they stand in awe in front of the three or four six-foot-high wonders. I love them with all my heart and they love me right back. They never leave the store to pick up disease or germs and are always there to do their job. They keep the humidity level in a comfortable range and also help to reduce the static in winter.

So if you can't bring people to their senses, by all means send me some seeds. I will give them a loving home among others that are loved.

Tom

Dear Arthur:

Re: Mexican Hat plant

PLEASE send me one of the offspring of your plant. I'm enclosing a SASE — to a Winnipeg address, rather than to Yellowknife, because I will be there from Dec. 16 to Jan. 10, and I would hate to expose the poor thing to even more inhospitability than it has already experienced by CBC!

When I moved from Winnipeg to Yellowknife last January, I took pieces of all my plants in my luggage, and transplanted them once I arrived. They thrived beautifully in the summer's twenty-hour sunlight, but are shutting down during these last few weeks when we have about five hours of daylight — with not much sun.

Would you report, on your show, the numbers of listeners that sent in requests . . . and how many you were able to fulfill?

Linda Bruce

December 15, 1992

Dear Arthur:

I am writing to request you send me a few Black Beauty seeds from which I intend to sow my own memento of "Basic Black."

Alas, more important matters concern me at present, however. Arthur, what is to become of your much-loved postal code? Not being totally fluent in Toronto geography I am only guessing that the move to the new CBC building will take you out of the wiener zone. This troubles me greatly because not all postal codes are great postal codes, and I worry that the new one won't live up to its esteemed predecessor.

I suggest that you tell us listeners what we have to work with, and begin a contest to christen the new code as soon as possible!

Happy Holidays,
Michele Kerschbaumer

December 12, 1992

Dear Arthur & Black Beauty:

What a lovely idea — to share your plant's progeny with your Saturday morning audience, who may well be as legion as Black Beauty's offspring . . . er Saltspring? (Cisco Kid's sombrero dangles indeed! — love it, having had one of these lovelies myself once, in my tiny West End apartment in Vancouver . . . who knows, maybe B.B.'s cousin?)

We would be happy to welcome the wee plantlet into our old farmhouse and our own arboretum, including the ceiling-high ficus my retired-farmer father prunes on his annual visit, and a Norfolk pine who prompts cracks like "Got your tree up, I see" from summer visitors anticipating Christmas.

Not to put too fine a point on it, your story of CBC's new building telling the people who will inhabit it how to live (didn't we humans used to be in charge?) struck a chord . . . enough to make me write. Your editorials usually do; I guess this time I was just close to a pen.

Arthur, thanks for a *great* show; you're a member of our family every Saturday morning! From a fan and friend and fellow Luddite,

Lindi Pierce

December 15, 1992

Dear Arthur:

CBC Broadcast Centre management's anti-plant policy would be a fitting topic for an "As It Happens" investigative piece. Alternatively, it might be the perfect opportunity for Scoop Jordan who, for all I know, has been unemployed since the "Radio Show" folded.

I will be very pleased to receive some seeds from Black Beauty, at least one for the office, its natural habitat, and one for home, where I listen to "Basic Black." That way, I can attempt to determine whether the plant responds primarily to an office environment or the sound of your voice.

Sincerely,
Dennis Peters

P.S. Sending a plant is a common way of expressing congratulations on the achievement of a major objective. If any senior managers in the Centre received any such living gifts when the Centre opened, you may have all the precedent you need. Just compose a congratulatory note on your move (from an anonymous fan, of course), put a big bow on the plant and have a courier deliver it to your new digs!

Dear Arthur:

Since there are no computers or microchips of any kind to protect from viruses and microbes in my naturally well-lit office — only people — I think I can provide a suitable caring home for a progeny of your ill-fated plant.

My condolences on your losses. Please don't stop broadcasting. We (poor helpless patients — and staff) love your program even if scalpel control on Saturday mornings is a bit difficult at times.

Best Regards,
Peter R. Wooding, D.D.S.

December 12, 1992

Dear Arthur:

I listened with heavy heart on December 12th as you described your plant dilemma and though you called Black Beauty a beast, I thought I heard a catch in your voice as you offered its seed pods up for general adoption. Please be assured that with me any offspring of Black Beauty will find all the comforts a dispossessed houseplant could hope for. It will have no shortage of company as I have a rather significant number of houseplants. Curiously, I have never actually had to buy a plant to create this collection. They have all been gifts or salvages. Starting with a mongrel frond I rescued from a garbage basket in residence at the University of Toronto, I have recycled and redeemed a menagerie of potted pals. A curious little potted tree was left permanently in my custody by a sorrowful, departing owner who could not carry it on in her adventures. A fussy burro's tail was given to me by my grateful, green-thumbed brother as a thank-you gift and it has been in intensive care ever since. Three little creeping plants which were left to their own devices at my in-laws' home are here now; their tendrils have grown together and re-rooted, making three plants into one unwieldy leafy unit.

Every plant taken in to this foster home of flora gets plenty of water, Dr. Schwartz's plant food, sunlight, TLC and *a name.* No plant is anonymous. We have, to introduce a few, Lieutenant Pappy, the Papyrus, Bowington and a dish of cacti named, after books of the New Testament, Acts, TimTim, Titus, Phlip, and Philemon. (These are currently suffering from an Old Testament–type plague and their fates are sadly doubtful.) The cedar bush on our balcony is, of course, Peter the Cedar. Spider plants have presented a particular challenge. The originals were Marlowe, Peele, and Our Man Shakespeare. Their offshoots have quite nearly exhausted the list of major Renaissance dramatists. Fortunately there were quite a number of lesser-known contemporaries, but I suspect we will eventually have to move into the Restoration period to christen the spider descendants to come.

At any rate, to this assortment of waywards and strays, I would be happy to add a new member, especially one from "Basic Black." Your show provides a multitude of possible names: George St. John Quinby? Baby Beauty? Baby Black? Harold F.? This will require some thought indeed.

Of course, I couldn't write soliciting a seed from Black Beauty without thanking you for many hours of delight and instruction in the esoteric aspects of life and human history. Your program is an integral part of our Saturday morning routine. I also would say that along with a collection of plants, I also have a collection of books, all of which came with their own names, which I am equally eager to augment. Please drop this letter into the "Basic Black" mail bin and pull it out again soon!!

Thanks for your time. Good luck with the move and the new studio.

Arleane Ralph

December 12, 1992

Dear Arthur:

Your offer of a man-eating Black Beauty seed has moved me to write to you. We live in the Interlake district, north of Winnipeg, so watching something grow green in the winter would be a delight. If B.B. is as robust (and handsome) as you say, it should be able to hold it's own against our dog-eating cat, Spike.

I've often thought about writing to tell you how much I enjoy your show, but frankly, couldn't be bothered until you offered something free. If you don't have a seed available, could you send me something else?

Your faithful fan,
Susan Rysar

P.S. I really do enjoy your show very much, and will continue to be an avid listener, even if you stiff me.

Expectantly yours, S.R.

Dear Arthur:

Please forward some seeds from your "unwanted by the CBC" plant. I had one of these years ago, but its care lost out to the kids and the dog. Now that the dog (eighteen years) has died and the kids have left home, I'd like to try one again. Thanks.

Mrs. (Mona) Pachal

December 12, 1992

Dear Arthur:

I would be honoured to give one of Black Beauty's offspring a home. In a few days I will receive my Master of Library Science degree, with no prospect of employment. This means two things:

1) I'll have plenty of time to care for the plant;

2) If something goes wrong with it, I'll know how to find a book about the problem!

(Oh, and I'll be able to catch "Morningside" every day now.)

I love "Basic Black" — keep it up!

Nancy Crozier

That's No Sexual
Innuendo —
It's Just a Fig
Leaf of Your
Imagination

*L*ife is cruel. Here I am on the far side of the half-century mark, and I still haven't written an opus of erotica. I always meant to. I sensed that Canada was ready for a *Portnoy's Complaint*, a *Fanny Hill*, a *Lady Chatterley's Lover* — maybe even a *Memoirs of a Canadian Casanova*.

Yeah, you're right. In my dreams.

Fortunately, Canadian culture will not suffer for my dismal performance in the fields of LoveLit. Once again, "Basic Black" listeners took up the slack, proving that there's still a sufficiency of hormones rocketing around in the Great White North. Herewith, a titillating peek under the covers, as provided by the folks who tune in (when they're not, ah, busy) to "Basic Black."

Don't leave this section where the children might find it.

Dear Arthur:

Poor Arthur, what you know about navels wouldn't fill a bat's belly button. Useless? Far from it. Navels have aesthetic, spiritual, and sensual functions that you have sadly neglected. First, aesthetic. Look east, Arthur! Navels have been adorned with precious stones for millennia. Mine might not look so hot with a ruby or a sapphire in it, but many is the belly button that provides a better setting for a jewel than any gold ornament could provide. Now, spiritual. What about navel gazing? Has mankind ever developed a more enlightened occupation than navel gazing? I think not — except perhaps for exploring the sensual aspects of the navel.

Arthur, my wife is possessed of one of the great belly buttons in this world. Not only is it in exactly the right place, it's also deep. Very deep. Large enough to hold more than a thimbleful of champagne or even cognac. This amazing virtue has earned my wife's navel the moniker "the shot glass of heaven." Arthur, you haven't truly lived until you've sampled your favourite spirit from the navel of your loved one.

Yours in navel gazing,
Jim Blackburn

April 27, 1992

Dear Arthur:

I am one of your faithfully sporadic listeners. Saturdays are busy days in my household, so I listen to you in odd moments snatched from garden-digging, grocery-shopping and dog-from-cat-separating. If I had a garage and a tobacco habit, I would listen to you behind the former while indulging in the latter in furtive schoolboy delight.

Anyway, in a moment of guilty pleasure this Saturday past, I happened to catch the last part of your monologue on navels, and as you claimed to know only one interesting thing about them, I thought I'd pass on two more in return for the hours of amusement you've given me.

First, did you know that an American armed forces pamphlet was briefly banned because it contained a drawing of Adam and Eve with navels? It's true.

The pamphlets were intended to encourage GIs from radically different backgrounds to get along with each other in the melting pot they had been pitched into by the draft in World War II. To make the point that we are all part of the same family, the producers of the pamphlet had included the offending illustration.

The whiff of blasphemy tickled the nostrils of some moss-backed congressmen from the Deep South.

They launched a drive in some House committee to have the pamphlet withdrawn, claiming it impugned the majesty of the Almighty by implying He created something with no earthly (or heavenly) use, that is, belly buttons. These politicians were apparently maintaining a belief that had slouched along the shady fringes of theology since the Middle Ages, that Adam and Eve were created perfect and hence without seemingly superfluous navels. The challenge to the pamphlet was eventually shot down, but not before religion had once again been pressed into the service of intolerance.

The real objection to the pamphlet was more sinister than mere quibbles over Genesis. The pamphlet had asserted the equality of the races of man, which was still a controversial notion in Alabama in the 1940s. The congressmen at least had the grace to be ashamed enough of their bigotry to use the umbilicated Adam as a stalking-horse.

In truth, I suppose a fellow created from dust would have had no umbilical cord and thus no navel, but then when did we get them? Did Adam look down when he was expelled from the Garden and discover he had been cursed with one? Did he hitch his newly-stitched fig leaves higher to try and hide it, as some men comb side-hair across a bald spot? Or did the mark of infamy only appear in his children, causing him to cast dark glances at Eve and wonder if there had been Fuller Brush men lurking in Paradise? You can find the story of the congressional controversy (which my memory has probably garbled) in a witty book by Bergen Evans called *The Natural History of Nonsense*. I unfortunately lent my copy out to someone and can't give you the publisher, but I think it was printed about 1967 under the Vintage imprint.

The navel also crops up, or rather dimples in, in another artistic context. The syndicates that distribute comic strips in the United States employ, or used to, an editor who rejoiced in the title of "pecker checker." It was his job to screen all strips submitted to ensure that no characters held brooms, bottles or Bren guns at angles that might produce an unintentionally phallic effect. He also checked for navels.

Why they were deemed offensive is puzzling. Maybe they were too earthy, too insistently physical for the sanitized world of the Sunday funnies. At any rate, Mort Walker, the creator of Beetle Bailey, was adamant in drawing navels on his characters whenever the occasion demanded it. Each time he did, the navels were excised by a drudge with a razor blade at the syndicate offices. Word got back to Walker that one editor had a collection of his expurgated navels in what he called the "Beetle Bailey Belly-Button Box." Eventually Walker submitted a strip that I think took place on a beach with navels on everything in sight, including oranges. The mass navelectomy required would have reduced the drawing to the texture of fine lace, and the censor gave up in despair. He never bothered Walker again. By such struggles have we achieved the freedoms we take for granted today.

I read of the affair in Mort Walker's book *Backstage at the Strips*, which concerns the life and habits of syndicated cartoonists, who on his account behave like the characters in a Peter de Vries novel. I lent my copy out to a brother who keeps finding excuses not to return it, so I am again unable to give you any bibliographic data.

I hope these stories will add to your store of navel lore. I happen to think that belly buttons are important. So did the ancient Greeks. Their word for navel was "omphalos." A boulder called the Omphalos stood on the sacred heights at Delphi to show that this was the centre of the world.

Why I can remember this sort of trivia when really useful information like how to fix a bike tire or pacify an irate spouse slips through my head like quicksilver puzzles me. I can only think that as Blake could see eternity in a grain of sand, and David Suzuki can gather intimations of the grandeur of the universe from fruit flies, little trifles like those above allow lesser minds like mine glimpses of the strange and silly richness of humanity. Or it may just be that my brain, like my navel, gathers fluff.

At any rate, Arthur, keep turning your gaze on the subjects that are central to us. I enjoy your show immensely. Long may you keep us all from our Saturday chores by doing yours.

Yours sincerely,
Geoff Snow

Dear Arthur:

Each of us indulges in certain daily or weekly rituals. For me, Saturday mornings consist of coffee, the morning paper and, of course, "Basic Black" on the radio. I cannot imagine those mornings without absorbing snippets of the obscure, inane and frequently bizarre. Not to mention the fact that I've grown very fond of the dulcet tones of George St. John-Quimby on a biweekly basis. I was introduced to this weekly compendium by my significant other, a displaced Maritimer with impeccable taste in ties (see enclosed picture).

This, however, brings me to the main reason for this letter. Sometime ago, in December I believe, you mentioned that you deplored the term "significant other." After long and careful consideration, I am hard-pressed to find anything better. The term "boyfriend" is distinctly adolescent in flavour. "Gentleman companion" brings to mind some individual with vaselined hair, patent leather shoes and a penchant for the tango. I suppose I could call him an "inamorato" or even a "paramour" but this summons up images of illicit liaisons at some place called "The No-Tell Motel."

I am told that the U.S. Dept. of Internal Revenue has a term known as a P.O.S.S.L.Q. Or rather, "Person of Opposite Sex Sharing Living Quarters." As a matter of fact, I believe humorist Mark Russell penned a charming little ditty entitled "Won't you be my POSSLQ?" But this won't work for us because even though he is (of the opposite sex) we're not (sharing living quarters).

A friend of mine refers to hers as "my commitment." A professor of mine, who goes out of his way to avoid gender specific language, has a "sweetie." I've even heard of people referring to their loved one as an "attaché." But I'm not sure that I like the idea of being intimately involved with a briefcase or similar carry-on luggage.

The sad fact is, Arthur, modern terminology just hasn't caught up with lifestyles. This has left a great many of us older, unmarried, not-living-in-yet-romantically-involved people out in the proverbial cold. So, until language catches up, be assured that it is better to be a significant other than an insignificant other any day of the week.

Yours truly,
Leslie G. Gratton

December 12, 1992

Dear Arthur:

I enjoyed your show this Saturday. In your talk with the author of *You Won't Believe Your Eyes*, he mentioned that the pupils dilate when their owner is aroused. Interestingly, Desmond Morris, in his book *People Watching*, reported a study in which men were asked to choose between two apparently identical photos of a young woman's face. In fact, one photo had been retouched to enlarge the pupils, and this photo was preferentially chosen as being the more attractive. So it would appear that your average male has this knowledge about the "window of the soul" wired into his brainstem, which is lucky, since women have been around longer than books.

But men aren't the only ones to know about this quirk. Women in some places used to place atropine drops in their eyes to dilate them and hence look more attractive to unwitting males who apparently seem to operate at the brainstem level in these matters.

The atropine was derived from a plant commonly called "Belladonna," meaning "Beautiful Woman." Fascinating, eh?

Speaking of plants, I'd love one of your "Black Beauty" seeds, so I've enclosed an envelope as asked.

Thanks!

Roberto Rouget

Dear Arthur:

I listened with great interest (as usual) to your Feb. 8 show and in particular to your piece comparing men and women, I missed the name of the woman to whom you were speaking about this fascinating topic (also the damn phone no. I was to call with the following vital information!).

Aside from the obvious biological differences such as the fact that men's underarm perspiration has significantly more "nose" than a woman's (of comparable physical and social stature), and that a deodorant designed *specifically* to over-power the more aggressive masculine stink molecules but moulded into a shape that to the untrained eye is only minute-ly different from that of a male "stick" but yet that seemingly insignificant difference renders the female "baton" *completely unusable* and presumably *ineffective* in a male "pit," and the well-known yet puzzling inability of a female cigarette smok-er's first and second fingers to spread open as wide as her male counterpart! For anyone who has attended doctor school this condition is indeed a mystery, for while both genders' digits appear to be constructed in the same fashion and from like material, the male cigarette smoker's number one and number two fingers spread far enough apart to allow, nay, to necessi-tate, the placement of the burning bundle in the very crotch of the two aforementioned pinkies.

The female smoker's hand appears to be less articulated in this regard as the extent of "finger spread" is greatly reduced compared to that of the male leaf smoker, the result being that the offensive smouldering tube is grasped approximately 25 mm from the tips of the fingers, which also seems to cause a strange type of temporary paralysis, for the fingers also seem unable to bend until the offending object is expelled — at which point full use of the hand is restored.

Now for a little-known but equally puzzling gender inequity. Crooked bread slicing! Yes, most women have an awful time slicing bread straight (the plane of the slice perpendicular to the longitudinal axis of the loaf), while most male toast mechanics produce slices that are perhaps not geometrically perfect but to the untrained eye are "square" to the loaf and are readily accepted by most toasters of the "drop and slot" design and are eagerly jettisoned when the predetermined degree of brownness is obtained.

Women on the other hand tend to produce "wedges" or at best "parallelograms" or a combination of the two, both of which are totally unacceptable as toaster fodder, and if one was able to brown one of these shapes it would prove itself completely useless, as a poached egg placed upon it would certainly roll right off of it and possibly onto the floor. While these "slices" might make good doorstops or perhaps "height elevators" in short people's shoes, they make mighty poor foundations for french toast or sandwich makings. Now the reason for the difference in slicing ability is simple: men, while slicing, look down on the loaf being dissected; women, however, hold their head tilted to one side and look at the END of the loaf as they cut. Why? Perhaps it is some primordial urge or an obscure maternal instinct, we may never know, but if it had not been for the advent of the automatic bread slicer or prepackaged, presliced, extruded bread as we now know it, that marvellous chrome-plated, watt-consuming, bread-bag-melting device that we share our breakfast table with might have gone the way of the yo-yo and our lives would be a little less meaningful.

Sincerely,
Keith Matheson

April 20, 1992

Dear Arthur:

You recently did a phone-in on the show about the differences between men and women and I enjoyed that very much. It's time to put those petty things aside now, to try to overcome our differences. In the spirit of true post-New-Age understanding, compassion and cooperation I would humbly like to suggest an item on similarities between men and women. Here are a few suggestions.

Men and women both think they are intellectually superior/better drivers, etc., etc. These types are pretty obvious.

Men and women both think the dog loves them best.

A man and a woman will both think the other is infinitely superior at grocery shopping, painting and wallpapering.

Men and women both think they do more than their fair share of housework.

When the baby cries at 3:00 a.m. both parents will think it is crying for the other.

Both men and women think in-laws should not necessarily be invited.

Men and women both spend a lot more time thinking about orgasm than they spend actually experiencing it.

Thanks Arthur. It's not Saturday without your show.

Yours sincerely,
Michael Nitsch

November 6, 1989

Dear Arthur:

Thanks for your card acknowledging my letter (copy attached to jog your memory). I have heard from a friend of a friend, etc., that you read the first kiss story on your program during the summer (I don't know how I missed your show . . . I must have been on holidays or sleeping after night shift or . . .).

Anyway if you did read it, I'm truly flattered and would really appreciate getting a tape of it so I can brag to my grandchildren. Is this possible? If so, and if there is any cost involved, let me know and I will send money right away!

Thanks a lot!

Dear Arthur (I listen to your show enough to dispense with "Mr. Black"):

I felt I had to write to you after your June 3 show featuring pet stories and a call for "first kiss" stories as I have what I think are amusing tales on both subjects. First, though, I would like to point out to you a couple of things we have in common. I just received my first copy of the Oakville *Beaver* in which my "Canadian Crossword" appeared for the first time, and I see you have a column in it as well. The second thing is the subject of one of your columns — Saltspring Island. I quite enjoyed this as I lived on Saltspring for my high school years through the early '70s. Most of us kids would talk about where we would go and what we'd do there to seek our fame and fortune once we left "the Rock." Staying there was not really an option I considered, but, you guessed it, I would love to be able to move back there now, and, hearing your column, know that no explanation is necessary.

Anyway, on to my stories. The first takes place on Saltspring and the subject is our independent cocker spaniel, Barney. In his younger days, Barney had been diagnosed by a vet as being oversexed (I still can't figure out what that had to do with his problem of constipation, which he was seeing the vet for). Barney and I were the same age, 14, when this episode took place. He had been missing for about three days and the family sort of resigned ourselves to the high possibility that Barney, in his frail and deaf condition, had met his demise at the wheels of a car he couldn't hear. I was calling my Dad from a phone booth in town for a ride home after scuba lessons, when I turned around to see four dogs, single file, traipsing down the main street of Ganges, a female in heat in the lead, followed closely by Barney, then two much younger and less experienced males. I retrieved Barney without too much resistance. I guess he was a bit tired by now, anyway, and seeing me, figured he could get a ride the four miles home. That was Barney's last amorous adventure that we know of, as he went to doggie heaven the following summer. (He was not, contrary to rumour, shot by a jealous husband.)

I met the subject of my kiss (not *first* kiss) story in a bar here in Regina. We hit it off quite well from the beginning and talked and drank the night away. I gave her a ride home on my motorcycle and, right under her parent's bedroom window at about 2 a.m., leaned over to give her a goodnight kiss. Finding this a little difficult with my full-face-shield helmet still on, I lost my balance and went straight over sideways, pinning my left leg under my 200+-pound bike. Not too impressive, but what followed was. She only laughed at my predicament a little, then proceeded to lift this hunk of metal off me with an almost perfect clean-and-jerk (me being the jerk). I was so taken by this feat of strength, I married this girl five short months later. That was eleven years ago, and just yesterday she continued to amaze me with a demolition job to make room for a deck in the backyard.

That's all for now, Arthur.

Sincerely,
Rick McConnell

September 23, 1989

Dear Arthur:

I'd love an autographed copy of your book and figure the following true story is worth one.

I was twelve years old and on my way home from school. Walking behind me was Tommie Gilchrist, the boy of my dreams. It was even hard for me not to shake when I knew he was within twenty feet of me. That day he was probably fifteen feet behind me. Well it so happened that I ran out of underwear that day, so I decided I'd borrow a pair of my mum's underpants. I wore my white pleated skirt with its elastic waist band and rolled the very large, silky underpants into the band. Well, as the day wore on the underpants became more and more detached from the waist band. I was only four houses away from my home when I could feel the underpants creeping down to my knees. But Tommie Gilchrist was behind me so I wasn't going to stop. The next thing I knew the underpants had fallen to the sidewalk. I just walked out of them to my home. The underpants lay on the ground.

After that day I decided I didn't like Tommie Gilchrist anymore.

Helen Murphy

The Grab Bag

So many letters, so little time. For a few years I kept each and every letter that came in to "Basic Black." They filled a file folder in no time. Then a whole drawer in my filing cabinet. Then the whole filing cabinet.

Pretty soon I was stuffing them in Glad bags and kicking them under the desk, behind my bookcase, up against the window.

I began tucking surplus sacks of them in my producer's office when he was off in the cafeteria. I just couldn't throw them away.

But I had to. It was that, or rent them a hotel room.

That's when the brains of the operation — my partner, Lynne Raymond — came up, as she so often does, with the solution.

"Why don't you put the best ones in a book?" she suggested. "You could call it *Blackmail!*"

Err, yeah.

So that's how this book came to be. And finally, we come to the tail end of *Blackmail!* and we still have these letters that don't quite fit any of our categories. Solution: give them a category of their own; they're too good to waste. Here's the "grab bag" — being a compendium of miscellany examining sundry topics ranging from hairpieces to Lotusland, underwear, and Her Majesty the Queen.

Enjoy!

And don't forget to write.

February 16, 1991

Dear Arthur:

I've been a regular listener to your show for some time now, and I've reached the conclusion that you and Harold Fisk are one and the same person. In fact, CBC Radio has deliberately perpetuated this cruel (and somewhat disgusting) hoax for years in order to save paying the salaries of two over-priced radio personalities.

So come on, Arthur/Harold, 'fess up! If you choose to continue to hoodwink your listening faithful, I defy you to *prove* that your split personality actually exists in two separate bodies. And don't try any of that trick radio stuff, like having both voices talking at the same time — I know you CBC guys have enough electronic equipment on board to sink the *Queen Elizabeth II*.

Yours sincerely,
Chris Denholm

P.S. If you have an extra copy of your book, feel free to send it my way.

Hiya Arthur:

Well, you've had your gloat. You teased poor Marg Mikol (Sp?!?) with your oh-so-sympathetic questions, snickering up your sleeve the while: "Aw, poor Lotusland had a few inches of snow dropped on it, did it? Gee, that's too bad — so tell us, Marg, just how unprepared were you guys for these flurries? Just how desperate and woebegone do Vancouverites look after a few days of *real* weather?"

All right. Yes, we had a snowstorm last week — dismissively brushed off by the rest of Canada as "a few flurries." And yes, you'd have to go a long way to find a more flummoxed being than a Vancouver native faced with a few flakes of the cold white stuff that don't melt upon landing.

But — I hope you had a really good, enjoyable gloat — because, judging by the winters past and the law of averages, that gloat's going to have to last you another twenty years or so. I hear rumours that Toronto's been getting its share of the white stuff lately, while in these parts the snow we received last week had been vanishing rapidly. The snowmen are taking a last stand, but for the most part the snow has retreated to out-of-the-way corners, where it huddles, sulking, in dirty piles.

While Canada defrosts, Vancouver and Victoria will be enjoying a wet, warm spring. And this year, we'll be grinning twice as broadly as usual, and sending twice as many photographs to relatives out East.

Go ahead and gloat, Arthur! It's not as if you don't have reason; we get some pretty good laughs too, watching our neighbours cope with snow. Besides, if your snickers ever get irritating, we simply console ourselves with the thought of the months to come, when the snow will only be an unpleasant memory and all you lot will be griping enviously to yourselves, and muttering about moving West.

Because the fact is, though we don't laugh last about the weather, we do laugh longest.

. . . On other matters, I have been enjoying "Basic Black," as usual. But I think you might have a small problem with regards to the — shudder — loathsome Harold Fisk. (Ick!) While honesty is essential, and I'd be the last person to suggest that you lie on the air, you might want to consider being less vehement in your denunciations of Harold. Even though he is all too closely linked to the gutter-press, you might be advised to — ah — downplay this regrettable fact a bit.

If not, if the repulsion you feel for him is too strong to be suppressed, then you should at least think about answering one small, niggling question, to wit: Why is a fine, upstanding show like "Basic Black" allowing its airtime to be sullied by the likes of that slimeball, Harold Fisk? If you don't give a good, clear answer to this question, then I'm afraid you leave your listeners to draw conclusions of their own: dark, unpleasant conclusions, which you'd probably rather refute.

Something to think about. . . .

Anyhoo, 'stime I signed off, I guess. Thank you muchly for the postcard you sent a month or two back; it gave me great cachet (or something like that . . .) in certain CBC-listening circles. Please don't put this letter in the draw for yer book, since I already have a copy.

Be happy,
Peregrin
(Sara Brearley)

February 9, 1991

Dear Black:

During a violent spring wind and rain storm a few years ago a stack of plastic milk cases stacked outside the local grocery store ended up strewn across the parking lot and adjacent side street. Coming out of the store into a deserted parking lot, I couldn't resist loading a few into the hatch of my Toyota. I had *no* milk cartons — everyone else seemed to; these, I rationalized, were flotsam anyway, a hazard to navigation on the side street. I loaded a few more, for a good solid Toyota load of about eight. A self-righteous (sanctimonious even) passerby gave me a disdainful "Oh come on!" And there the guilt started. Driving home, it seemed as if everyone I passed on that rainy night stared at my load of loot. I got home, drove around back and skulked in the back door with carton after carton. Piled in the kitchen. The guilt was coming to a head, approaching hysteria. I (honestly!) imagined the police coming to the door. The whole load ended up in my attic, minutes later. Minutes after that, I was back in the grocery store parking lot, dumping all eight back where they came from. I still have no milk cartons, but a clear conscience.

Good work! (Occasionally),

Don Clark

Dear Arthur:

Somewhere in central Australia, near Ayers Rock, there's a little community that has what must be the hardest water in the world. This water does something amazing to the average bar of soap. Instead of sudsing up into nice cleansing bubbles, the bar of soap gets soft and gritty. It sort of resembles a bar of lard with sand mixed in. Let me tell you how I found out about this.

I was on a bus tour of central Australia, and we were stopping overnight in this little place. After spending a rousing evening in the bar I decided to take a quick shower before I went to bed. About halfway through the shower I noticed that the soap had a peculiar gritty texture. Then I noticed that the soap wasn't lathering. I started rubbing harder and faster in an attempt to work up a lather. (Big mistake.)

By the time I had realized that this soap was *not* going to lather, half of my body, and my hair, was covered with this lard-like substance that was *not* rinsing off. I ended up scraping off as much of it as I could. The next day it was off to the desert again. As we bounced along the outback roads the bus would fill with dust, every grain of which would cling to my sticky coating. By the second day out I had developed dreadlocks, and to look at things on the positive side, I had developed a coating of grime which rendered me impervious to sunburn. At night I lined my sleeping bag with newspaper to prevent it from getting as disgusting as I was. Finally, after close to a week out in the desert we came to another little community where a shopkeeper told me the secret of washing in ultrahard water, dish-washing liquid. That was the only thing that would work. So I bought a bottle of Joy and spent the next hour slowly scrubbing off my lard/mud/sweat/coating that I'd been trapped inside for close to a week, and that's my Frankenstein travel story.

Pat Fuller

Dear Arthur:

This morning I heard your conversation with a young woman who experimented with winter camping. My husband and I did that years ago, too. We had to sleep outside in the dead of winter within sight of the cabin of a ski resort. Our shelter was a piece of plastic. Were we crazy or what? Having survived that ordeal and fumbled through an introduction to orienteering the next day, we eventually went on to bigger and better things.

We shipped our little car to Europe and camped for an entire year, covering most of Great Britain, Western Europe and parts of North Africa. When we camped in the Lake District, our campground was a lake . . . We awoke to find the plastic floor of the tent undulating. There was a good two inches of water under it. When we pitched our tent on the edge of the Sahara Desert in Morocco, it rained for the first time in three years and we were hailed as heroes.

I quickly realized that there were many situations when I would feel neither safe nor comfortable venturing forth from the tent in the dead of night in order to pee. (Is this vulgar? I think the camping women of the world who have not worked out a solution to this should be privy to this idea, pardon the pun.) At the beginning of the trip, when we actually had more than $2.00 discretionary cash, my husband bought a two-litre plastic bottle of pop. When he finished the pop, I kept the bottle, thinking we could use it for extra water. Well, necessity is the mother of invention. One day I was sitting in the tent wondering how I could transform my anatomy in order to successfully use the bottle for "night-time number one." I happened to glance at a plastic funnel we used to fill our primus stove with fuel. Voila! When a lady positions herself directly over a funnel, and positions the funnel tube in the mouth of a container, she has the neatest contrivance ever.

For the rest of that year, I never had to make pee-pee trips in the night. But I didn't have the nerve to tell our camping acquaintances about my invention, either. Indeed, my husband won't even allow me to use my last name, which is double and includes his. I have to revert to my maiden name and risk eternal banishment by my older daughter just to pass on this helpful hint. It's worth it, though, if it keeps a desperate traveller inside her tent at night.

Cheers,
Jennifer Smith

Hey Arthur, here's my road story . . . a bit late:

On the eve of my sixteenth birthday, I hit Highway 20 with all of $20 and not even a change of underwear for an initiatic pilgrimage that would take me around the Gaspé Peninsula in the pursuit of social recognition as a true member of the hippie generation.

After a week of such delicacies as ditch-sleeping and breadless peanut butter sandwiches, I hit rock bottom in Matane, 600 clicks short of home. I was facing starvation and humiliation if I did not get a lift soon . . .

I struck it lucky when a middle-aged couple I met in the youth hostel cafeteria offered a ride back in their plush Citroën DS. I was enjoying the smooth ride from the back seat and could almost smell Mom's shepherd's pie when the driver turned to me and anxiously asked, "Gee, doesn't it smell a bit like burnt rubber?" I am almost odour blind but this French car did smell a bit like French cheese! It got quite busy on the flight deck as the crew flipped every switch on the dash. Gears got shifted, brakes tested, radio and ventilation turned off to no avail. All windows were open but the smell seemed to always come back. We stopped on the shoulder to kick the tires and went on our way for another little while. We stopped again, and the driver hid behind the hood, only to emerge some time later with grease all over him and a pitiful look on his face; just couldn't find why his luxurious marvel was self consuming on the highway. My only worry was that I'd be late for supper.

After an hour of stop and go we finally checked in at a side-road garage to have a mechanic take a peek. I took advantage of the delay to walk a bit on the road and get some fresh air; we roadies can't sit still for too long. Here I was 300 feet away from the car, and I could still smell burnt rubber . . . burnt rubber . . . I look down at my feet; my old battered running shoes with 16,000 miles of rain and shine on them had split open, my unwashed feet overflowing on each side. I almost melted as I realized that French engineering was not at fault. I had never been so embarrassed in all my life. I threw the Adidas as far away as I could and hid in a ditch until the DS was gone in the sunset.

Well, there I was now, hitchhiking barefoot on cold concrete, with not even a dime to call Mom. Just like the Amex commercial without the Amex. Those would be the longest 600 miles I'd ever hitch. "Hey, I guess I better hit the road now . . . the soap . . ."

Peace man!

Denis Beaudoin

September 27, 1992

Dear Mr. Black:

I came across the following information while reading a book by David Attenborough: *Journeys to the Past.*

While travelling in New Guinea he came across an ancient ceremony which is remarkably like bungy/bungee jumping.

Here are the details, which might interest you. (It is, at least, a change from the Constitution!)

Bungy Jumping May Be Older Than We Think.

While on a Zoo Quest to Madagascar and other points . . . famed naturalist and explorer David Attenborough visited the Island of Pentecost in the New Hebrides, where he witnessed a ceremony which consisted of men and boys jumping from platforms situated at intervals down from the top of an eighty-foot tree. The jumpers were secured by vines tied around their ankles and sang as they jumped, each from his own platform.

The tree from which they launched themselves was lopped of its branches before the jumps, while singing men prepared the jumping platforms and braced the unstable tree with guy ropes. The women and children, who did not jump, encouraged the men and boys by dancing and chanting and whistling through their teeth.

Men who didn't have the courage to jump had to pay a fine in pigs. People interviewed by Attenborough had largely forgotten the meaning of the ceremony but some claimed the jump cured them of stomachaches and colds in the head.

The Attenborough books would be in most libraries.

Nicky Marchese

The Phoenix/Zephyrhills Parachute Center sits just on the edge
of town in the open countryside, next to the municipal airports.

As a newcomer to the area and a recent retiree, I was living
in a newly purchased mobile home about three miles from the
Jump Center but did not know of its existence until my next-
door neighbour's wife explained how "Jack" each morning
would go to watch them jump.

Parachuting has always held much interest for me. I am fas-
cinated by the perceived thrill of floating to earth under a
canopy of cloth. Parasailing, which I tried three years ago on a
beach in Mexico, was a poor substitute. Travelling as a passenger in a glider twelve to fifteen years ago was very enjoyable
but I still dreamt of some day floating to earth under a bil-
lowing chute.

My first day at the Phoenix/Zephyrhills Jump Center made
me aware of their offer, for $130.00 — a one-time "tandem
jump." I eagerly read the brochures and knew right then, I
would jump before I left for home at the end of my vacation.

When my wife and friends asked if I planned to jump, I was
noncommittal. I was not sure the authorities would allow me
to jump if it was necessary for me to divulge my history of
heart irregularity — I have an irregular heartbeat, one that
"races" and skips frequently. I realize the condition is common
but it can also be fatal.

A very close friend came to our park in early February to
stay for three months. Don is an ex-gunner on Halifax
bombers in World War II. On hearing of the Jump Center, he
immediately showed much interest and after his first visit, stated

162

his intention to jump. That was the encouragement I needed and I told him I too would jump. Don is 68 and I am 65. We made the arrangements.

On March 5, 1992, at 10 a.m., along with our wives and another couple from home, we arrived at the Jump Center. John and Grant, our instructors, welcomed us. The day was warm, about eighty degrees F, with light cloud but a strong NW wind. "Will the wind be a factor?" we asked. "Those jumpers going up now will let us know," they replied. In the meantime, we were instructed to fill out and sign five different disclaimer forms. Did we suffer from any serious illness? Heart disease? High blood pressure? Were we on any medications? To all of which we both answered no and promptly signed and initialled where so indicated.

The jumpers returned to earth and reported "no problem" with the wind. We were then summoned to the briefing office where John explained the jump and then, by video, showed us exactly how it would go. A reporter for the local paper made a tandem jump a month before, and the video was of him and his feelings of and interpretations of the jump. It looked very exciting.

Jump suits were issued along with a snug-fitting "helmet" and goggles. A harness was attached over the shoulders, around the middle and between the legs. It was pulled tight.

The instructors explained how we would be strapped to them, they to our back. The instructor wore the parachute. The proper way to exit the aircraft was explained and the position of the legs and arms during free fall was demonstrated. Lying on the floor, on the stomach, raise the legs, bend them at the knees spread-eagle fashion, at the same time raise your arms over the head and assume an arch in the back. We assured the instructors we knew what to do and could do it.

The announcement came over the loud speaker — Group #3 — thirty minutes to takeoff. That was us. Last-minute instructions on how to free-fall and we headed for the load area.

A ravine runs between the airport runway and the Jump Center. A small wood footbridge crosses the ravine and a sign at the bridge brought the whole idea of parachuting into perspective:

"Parachuting is a dangerous sport . . . If you are not prepared to accept that, do not go beyond this point." We continued to the launch area.

The aircraft, a Buffalo twin-engine rear-loading craft, came to life. Twenty-four jumpers milled around waiting for the signal to load. We were given one last instruction to be sure to assume the proper posture for a successful free fall. "OK, let's go," said my instructor and we all ran to the aircraft. As we were to jump last, we loaded first and took a position, seated on the floor, knees bent, legs apart so that the jumper ahead of you sat between your legs — everyone facing the rear of the aircraft.

Three rows of eight jumpers, all in a friendly light-hearted mood. I got a thumbs-up salute from the jumper beside me. A pat on the knee from the one in front. They knew we were a little nervous. They tried to reassure us.

We took off. At 7,500 feet five jumpers stood up. The rear hatch opened and one at a time, they stepped out backwards. Their chutes opened almost immediately. The hatch closed. Those five jumpers were Canadians from Alberta. Practising their specialty which is "stacking and rotating." By hooking their feet into the chute lines of the man below, they were able to "stack" one on top of the other. The rotating required the top man to drop down to the bottom position. This manoeuvre continued until the whole "stack" had dropped to within a few hundred feet of the ground. A tricky stunt and beautiful to watch.

At 13,500 feet the instructor behind me tapped my shoulder and said OK, time to go. We all stood up. The hatch opened and fifteen jumpers ahead of us left the aircraft in various styles and antics. I, with my instructor securely attached to my back, walked the twenty feet to the open hatch. We stood, toes overhanging, and looked out into space. Thirteen thousand, five hundred feet is a long way down. The sight was beautiful, the feeling *indescribable*. Because of my age, I thought all chance of reaching this moment had passed me by. I was absolutely elated. I remember someone counting — 1–2–3 — I fell forward. I was not prepared for the rush of wind that caught me. We tumbled and then I could detect the instructor reaching back to grab my leg and bend it back. I returned to reality, assumed the free-fall posture — legs spread, and bent at the knees, arms out and above the head, back arched — "push the hips out" as instructed.

We fell. Under those conditions the human body falls about 120 m.p.h. In tandem, the rate is about 200 m.p.h. Much too fast, so a drogue chute is deployed — a small billowy cloth ball to slow descent to about 120 m.p.h. And so we free-fell — I was rushing to the ground at 120 m.p.h. and could only think of how fortunate I was to be able to experience this thrill, which I was absolutely sure very few 65-year-olds would even consider, let alone achieve.

"WHOMP" — THE CHUTE OPENED. We stopped falling — with a jolt. No more, no less than I expected. The instructor insisted on the harness being tight — I am glad he did — we began to drift and I was shown how to direct the chute, from right to left and left to right. "OK," he said, "you're flying it." And so we descended. TOTAL time from exit to land: about five minutes (about fifty seconds of free fall). A total of 9,000 feet and four minutes of floating under the canopy.

The landing was as gentle as "stepping down." Ground crew assisted by collapsing the chute — the chutes used for tandem jumps are larger than regular chutes and with any amount of wind blowing they can create a hazard after the landing. It was a stand-up landing.

We walked off the field to the cheers of our wives and friends.

Congratulations were in order. A few minutes later, the public address system came to life: "Don Gandier and Sydney Turner have just completed their first tandem jump — Congratulations." We both felt very good.

Would I do it again? You bet. Will I? Not likely. As thrilling as the jump was, doing it at age 65 was a tremendous boost to self-assurance. I have always felt you are as young as you feel. I felt like a teenager that day.

NOTE

March 5, 1992, the day I jumped, was forty-seven years to the day my brother Ray died in the crash of his Lancaster bomber over England while on a bombing raid to Germany. He didn't have the opportunity to use his chute.

Sydney B. Turner

March 9, 1991

Dear Arthur:

I've been spending the last while drinking coffee, listening to your show, and avoiding writing a sermon. In other words a typical Saturday morning. And yet there is a difference. I'm still recovering from the shock I received in last week's show.

What shock, you might ask? The shock of discovering that one's hero has feet of clay. The disappointment of finding out that someone you have long considered to be a "kindred spirit" disagrees with you on a key issue. I am, of course, referring to your careless and disparaging remarks about singalongs.

You see, I loved singalongs in the car. My family passed many a mile singing what became family classics — "Little Sir Echo," "I'm a Lonely Little Petunia in an Onion Patch," "I'm a Nut," "Yabadaba" — the list goes on.

Furthermore, my love of singalongs is not just some happy memory of the past. I still love to sing in the car. This last summer, driving with my sister and mother between Edmonton and Regina, we sang through all the family classics and then launched into hymns, entire liturgies, and whole albums.

Perhaps, Arthur, all you need is to travel in the Johnson family car!

Love your show!

Yours fondly,
Susan Johnson

April 25, 1992

Dear Arthur:

While listening to your program this morning, I was quite surprised to hear you didn't know about carrageenin.

I live in western P.E.I. and fishermen, about fifteen miles from my home, for miles along the shore harvest Irish moss and sell it to companies. This company extracts the carrageenin which is used in ice cream, various puddings as well as milk shakes.

If you were to drive along the shore of P.E.I. in some areas you would see several horses at almost every homestead. These horses are used in the harvest of Irish moss. They are hitched into a kind of rake and are driven in the water along the shore to gather the moss. Some people pick it off the rocks along the shore.

Some is sold wet and some is spread on lawns and roadsides to dry.

I admit I didn't know how to spell carrageenin. I had quite a hunt through the dictionary and encyclopedia but I did find it and it is spelled correctly.

I enjoy your program.

Sincerely,
Alice Clements

September 30, 1989

Dear Arthur:

Enjoyed listening to your program on thoroughbreds' names. One criticism I must unload first.

People not connected usually with the horse business do not know the difference between a purebred and a thoroughbred. I feel sure you would not have taken on the program if you did not know that a thoroughbred is a breed — a racehorse. Purebred is a registered animal, not just horses.

Your question, does a name mean anything to the betting public? called for a wartime story. My air force girlfriend and I, stationed in London, England, in 1945, were on leave in Dublin. Getting off the bus in pouring rain, the conductor leaned over the back of the bus and whispered, "Put your money on 'Airborne.'" I knew it was a horse in the Derby the next day. Due to the rain, all we did was listen to the radio. Needless to say he won! And us nearly broke!! Anyway, we took off for Ascot the next day, won on "Steady Aim," and for a year we laid bets fairly successfully, because a name intrigued us.

One day, we picked a filly in a fourteen-horse race, because her name was "Heliotrope" — she won. The fellers in the Motor Transport section wanted to know our secret. My friend held out her tightly closed fist, like the punters on the track with a hot tip. Sergeant Dave, who took our bets, was not amused!

Sincerely,
Nancy L. Tegart
(Mrs. Lloyd Tegart)

February 3, 1991

Dear Arthur:

First of all let me thank you for being so prompt in sending Jan and I a copy of your latest literary chef-d'oeuvre. Given that it was the first time we ever won anything I promptly went out and bought a Lotto 6-49 ticket. Unfortunately our winning streak ended with your book. We wait until the triplets are down for the night then we use our much awaited sixty minutes of free time to read a few pages of *That Old Black Magic*. I was driving home after picking up our third crib (donated by friends of ours) when you read our letter over the air and as requested I'm enclosing a photo of our three little treasures. I've taken quite a few pictures with my trusty old Nikon but I must say, Arthur, our three little ones have proven to be my most challenging subjects yet (try getting three babies to smile at once!).

I hope you don't mind, Arthur, but we've made you an honorary uncle. So every Saturday a.m., between feedings and diaper changes, the whole household gets to listen to "Uncle Arthur's" program. Hopefully it will remain a tradition in our home for a long time to come. Well, parenting duties call, Arthur, but I'd like to close this brief note by extending an invitation to you and your family to visit us and the triplets if you're ever in "Winterpeg."

Take care and stay well,
Maurice Montreuil

February 29, 1991

Dear Arthur:

I always enjoy your show, but your piece on hairpieces finally prompted me to write. First, it served as a reminder that it is not only women that do amazing things in the name of beauty, and second, it provided the perfect opportunity to pass on my own cure-for-baldness story.

My family went to Scotland a few summers ago for a visit; my father has relatives over there that we had not seen in a number of years. We were being treated to lunch by one of my uncles when the merits versus faults of Sangster men playfully came up.

"Well," said my uncle, with his full head of hair, "at least Sangster men don't lose their hair . . ." His voice kind of trailed off as he then looked at his older brother's quite visible scalp (my father is after all in his seventies).

"Hmm . . ." he frowned and then wagged a finger at my father's forehead and advised, "You should rub some whisky on that! That's what we do for the sheep!"

I suspect that a liberal dose taken internally doesn't hurt either.

Thanks and keep up the great program,
Margaret Sangster

February 29, 1991

Dear Arthur:

While I am in letter-writing mode, I would like to put in my vote for a word that I would like banned. It was a quiet, unassuming and almost unheard word until one day, I think it was about two years ago, President Bush used it. I cannot remember anymore what he was referring to, but whatever it was, it was "not prudent at this time." And so the word prudent was dragged out of the closet and now appears in political speeches everywhere. Being or not being prudent has become the reason a politician uses when he/she cannot think of any better reason for doing or not doing the action in question. I have heard it used in statements on everything from international relations to mini-golf zoning. So I say, let's give prudent an extended vacation and hit the thesaurus. Let's see . . . that gives us discreet, wary, careful, cautious, wise and, what do you know — politic!

Thanks again,
Margaret Sangster

May 4, 1991

Dear Mr. Black:

I usually enjoy your program but occasionally some things are said that are inaccurate and that can be annoying when one trusts so much in the validity of what you speak about.

Today you were discussing hair and beard growth, linking them to light and the change of seasons.

I have a brother who inadvertently got a turkey drumstick stuck sideways in his mouth. Because he fears doctors it has remained there for several years. Because of this he drools a lot. To mask this he grew a beard. In one week he grew several inches of beard. Because of this I would suggest that it doesn't matter what the season is, what matters is what is in your mouth. It is drooling that causes growth. Most men with beards are probably sloppy eaters and secret droolers.

Also, light has nothing to do with hair growth. If that were so, all people wearing caps and hats would be bald. Then again, they may be. Ask everyone to take off their headgear and take a bow. That should settle that.

I am glad to have the opportunity to shed some light on this subject.

Yours truly,
Ronald J. MacDonald

Dear Mr. Black:

On a rebroadcast of a December 1988 program aired again July 29, 1989, you mentioned being accused of making fun of Peter Mansbridge's widow's peak. You pointed out you weren't doing any such thing because you yourself are balding.

This led me to wonder, what does he really look like? Often we conjure up pictures of people we hear on the radio or speak to on the telephone that we never actually meet, and when we do seldom does the fantasy live up to the reality.

I had pictured a tall, slender man with wavy brown hair, brown eyes hidden by tasteful wire-rim glasses, perhaps in his late thirties or early forties. This man, pictured to be you, wears a pale blue Arrow dress shirt and dark brown polyester slacks. He is a smoker who talks with his hands and has an annoying habit of pulling on his rather long chin. He is not quite hunk status, but not ugly either. How far off am I?

I too am a radio announcer and have also worked as a receptionist where my voice on the phone is my primary representation of myself. This whole business often makes me curious as to how other people see me. What do they think I look like? So I started to ask a few questions . . .

Another reporter whom I often spoke to in another city said I sound like a brunette. How, I asked, can a person *sound* like a brunette? He said I sounded too intelligent for a blond and too mellow for a redhead and too young to be greying.

An investment adviser who provided me with a daily stock report said I sound as though I have legs "that just don't quit."

I asked why he thought so, but he just **giggled** and would say no more.

The head of a company with whom my boss was trying to land a major contract claimed I sound like Kathleen Turner's sister. He went on to tell Bruce I was the most pleasant-sounding receptionist he'd ever heard and it would be a pleasure to do business with the company.

I often find telephone conversations with men go on longer than those with women in a business atmosphere and one of the first "chatty" questions asked is do I live alone.

After asking a number of people, both men and women, to describe me just by listening to my voice, they pegged me as a Paulina Poriskova type with a cascade of jet black curls, moist red lips, an ample bosom and a come hither look in my eye . . .

Ah, but truth is stranger than fiction. Alas, I look nothing like the supermodel for Estée Lauder, save the long brown hair. My looks are best described this way: "My sister is tall, thin and beautiful. I'm the opposite."

So, Mr. Black. What do you look like? What do those people you talk to every show look like that you've never seen . . . the operator helping you make an overseas call . . . the salesman with his book of wonderful coupons . . . the late-night disc jockey on your favourite station or the woman who calls to say your order is in from Sears . . . what about the people on distress lines or on 1-900 phone numbers?

Maybe I don't want to know what you look like after all. Sometimes it is fun to maintain an illusion. Perhaps you and I are the lucky ones because we can hide behind our microphones and telephones and no one really ever has to know we're balding or overweight or that we have on one brown sock and one green.

Sincerely,
Pauline M. Berrey

Dear Arthur:

Lawrence of Arabia was a truly outstanding film. I saw a matinée
and when I staggered out to the street with that post-movie
glaze, the blazing sun finished me off. I thought I was in a concrete desert. Saskatchewan in a dust storm in a convertible can
give you enough grit in your eye to make you cry too.

Once I found an old postcard of Lawrence in an antique
store and when my boyfriend saw it, he asked if he could send
it to his grandmother in England. She had been a friend and
neighbour of Lawrence. The poet Gerard Manley Hopkins was
in the vicinity. I saw a photograph of her estate. It was a block
long without a gable or arabesque or even a gargoyle, at least
on the outside. I bet you'd feel your rheumatism in a place like
that. Better to be sunblinded temporarily and dream of Arabia.

My mother has used this remedy for years with huge success. It's simple and cheap to prepare. Sulphur powder from a
drugstore, creamed in shortening or lard to make a salve, is the
best medicine for poison ivy and for diaper rash. I think Joan
Rivers should be kind (if it didn't make her too ill) and pass
that along to June Allyson.

You're right, Arthur, letters don't beget return letters like
they used to. This is not going to be a fat letter, for I have had
to resort to shovelling snow by moonlight. I'm keeping rather
Napoleonic hours, i.e., four hours of sleep and back to the
strategy. The battlefield is 300 metres long (about one fifth of
a mile) and it looks a little drunken because moonlit patches
are cleared while shaded areas remain pregnant with snow and

jewels. (Eldorado is near here.)

You've got your language bitches while I'm impacted by mindless people who call snow-shovelling a mindless thing. I do my best thinking there, and the snow flies when the invectives get downloaded, and tossed aside. I should think less and write more. I have an invitation to look at my letters that have been meticulously hoarded over the years and I'm sure they'll be revealing.

Merry Christmas to you all and your mice from me and mine.

Betty Gaos

P.S. I looked for Betty Fussil's corn book, but was unsuccessful. One can hardly find corn flour let alone exotic breeds in Canada. I'm cursed with celiac disease and that limits my grain to rice, and corn. Johnnycake recipes call for stone- and water-ground white corn. Cornbread, which I used to love, is mixed with wheat flour. There's no such thing as potato bread, and you can't really discern the potato content in the alleged potato bread.

Oh, well.

Dear Arthur:

"O Canada"

Oh Canada, our home and native man
You pick it up
We know our sons come in
With Gloria, we see your eyes
The two doors strong and freeze
From farmers' sides
Oh Canada, we stand on guard for me
God keep our man
Oh yes indeed
Oh Canada we stand on guard for Lee
Oh Canada we stand on guard for these.

This is how my wife says her Early Childhood Services class — kindergarten-age kids — sing our national anthem. It gave me a chuckle and in some ways its lyrics seem more appropriate than the "real thing."

We enjoy listening to your Saturday a.m. show on CBC. Andreas Schroeder was in the "Hat" recently and we had a short yak about literature — especially his excellent book *Dustship Glory* — and you. He says you're a fine fellow, even when the mike is off; but that could be two bearded wits covering for each other, eh?

Anyway, if you can use "O Canada" please do. My wife's name is Cathy Marco and she teaches E.C.S. at I. F. Cox Elementary School at Redcliff, Alberta, Canada.

Yours truly,
Ray Marco

May 28, 1991

Dear Mr. Black:

I wanted to write immediately after your Saturday program of Victoria Day weekend but spring is fast-lane around here. I doubt if you'll read it on the air anyway and I misplaced the phone number, but I have to tell you that you lost some listeners here after your pointless twaddle about a dedicated lady, Queen Elizabeth.

It made me rattle off the following:

Your pointless attack on the Queen
Was silly and petty and mean.
Befuddled she's not.
Must you stoop to the plot
Our Commonwealth head to demean?

Come on, Arthur B., why destroy something that has done such good?

Christine Pike

January 5, 1991

Dear Arthur:

I was listening to your show today and I heard a lady talk about children and weddings. It reminded me of a funny story a friend of mine told me.

My friend Pat was attending a wedding in which the bride had a child from a previous marriage. The little boy was running around the front of the church during the wedding ceremony. When the priest asked, "Do you take this man to be your husband?" the little boy yelled, "No!" The service had to be stopped for a few minutes because everyone was laughing so much.

I hope you enjoyed that as much as I enjoy listening to your show every week. (Who am I kidding? The story's not that good!)

Yours truly,
Wayne Peters

Dear Arthur:

I expect I'll be too late — still, never mind.

I know the topic for the week was superstitions, and I know I was supposed to phone the answering machine, but I couldn't — don't even begin to wonder why — and anyhow, I wanted to tell you about a graffito. So I'll keep my fingers crossed — will that count? Here goes.

I lived for a long time in Whitehorse in the Yukon, where I occasionally visited a hostelry you may even know, the Kopper King.

The doors on the cubicles in the ladies' loo there used to be cut rather high, some fifteen or eighteen inches above the floor. It was along the bottom of one of these doors — the second from the left, I recall — that, perched, I saw the most unnerving piece of graffiti a lady could imagine. It said,

"Beware of limbo dancers."

You light up our life. Well, our Saturday mornings, anyway. Thank you. Lots more, please.

Sincerely,
Anne Lloyd

Dear Arthur:

Let me tell you about my way of dealing with late essay excuses. My theory is that it doesn't hurt me as the instructor if an essay comes in late, but that it may be unfair to those students who do have their academic lives in order. So, I let the other students decide.

A few days before essays are due, any student who wants permission to go past the deadline has to stand up in front of the class and give his excuses, after which the class votes "yes" or "no" by secret ballot. Ballots are handed out carefully, as fraud has been known to occur.

Once a student brought a large portrait of a young woman — he explained that it was his girlfriend, who was in town from another university for just a few days, and that he would rather spend time with her than with his essay. He got almost unanimous approval. It turned out that the portrait was of his sister — he'd grabbed it off the piano as he left his parents' house that morning.

Occasionally bribes have been offered. One year a student abandoned his essay preparation to go out on a commercial fishing boat, earning several thousand dollars in two weeks — as soon as he let that fact slip out during his speech, he realized he was in trouble, so he offered every member of the class a free six-pack if the vote went in his favour. It did not.

Overall about two-thirds get their extensions, while the others lose out. Unfortunately, the smooth-tongued, smart-ass characters tend to do better than the shy serious types, but this fact provides another lesson from the real world of politics. And one last thing: you may have noted that I said "give *his* excuses." For some reason women students almost never try their luck in front of the class. Maybe they don't trust class politics; maybe they're better organized.

Anyway, Arthur, thanks for tapping into this vein of campus culture.

Sincerely,
Paul Tennant

Dear Arthur and crew:

I have not had a lot of luck with your answering machine of late so decided to trust my contribution to your "best excuses" call to Canada Post. I trust they can deliver it to you in time, without any excuses. The scene unfolds with me, a young air cadet, trying to exchange my torn trench coat for a new one.

"And how did you rip this?" the surly quartermaster demanded of me across his storeroom counter. I explained to the sergeant that my Royal Canadian Air Cadet standard issue trench coat received the damage in question in a most spectacular and hair raising fashion. The week before, my chauffeur, who was also Mom's much younger brother, had attempted his usual Wednesday night dash back and forth between our rural residence and the aerodrome. This had to be achieved in less time than it took the Toronto Maple Leafs to recuperate from period two and begin the third. The speed required was near twice the legal limit and drifting snow be damned. Fishtailing from side to side in that out-of-control souped up '55 Pontiac, I caught alternate glimpses of my neighbours' houses on one side of the road and the farmer's field on the other. I wasn't sure what would be the kinder ending, a trip though Phil Walmsley's living room window or a crash landing in Elmer Brown's corn stubble. The car chose the cornfield. Flashing through a gap in the roadside pole line, the Pontiac buried its nose into the snow-filled ditch, then brought its hind quarters over top. In all I counted several flips and as many rolls before vehicle and contents came to rest. Taking stock of the damage, we noticed a lack of windows, wheels, decorative trim and other details that help make a car a car. Mom's brother and I were fine, except where he had grabbed my trench coat during the aerial portion of our ride. Confident that this explanation had satisfied the quartermaster's enquiry and that surely I would be held blameless for the government's loss, I looked up, punctuating the end of my excuse with the most earnest expression a fourteen-year-old face could manage. After the briefest of contemplation the sergeant glanced down at the official form he was required to fill out and on its bottom line scribbled the word "fighting."

I enjoy your show, Arthur. Thanks for the invitation to participate.

Sincerely,
Tony Jenkins

Dear Arthur:

My "brush with fame" is a bit long and involved. If you think it interesting enough, maybe you would like to edit it and read it on air.

In 1949 I was a young Brit ex-serviceman managing a small hotel at a tiny place called Juba in southern Sudan, working for the Sudan Government Railways. I received a series of letters from Thos. Cook, the travel agent, telling me that Janet Gaynor, the movie star, was travelling in Africa with her husband, Adrian, the Hollywood dress designer. They were to arrive in Juba by station wagon from Kenya to catch the Nile steamer to take them downriver some 700 miles or so to Khartoum; coming in Saturday a.m. and sailing at crack of dawn on Sunday. Thos. Cook's instructions, repeated in several letters, were to provide them with everything and anything they wanted and to send the bill to Thos. Cook. I was at the jetty on the riverbank at the appointed time, introduced myself to Janet and Adrian, told them I was at their service for the day and waited for them to stow their luggage and to clean up a bit.

BUT — by the same transport also arrived two unaccompanied young ladies about my age. Canadian, apparently! One of them, an attractive brunette, caught my eye immediately and I would have dearly loved to spend the day dancing attendance on her instead of Janet Gaynor. However, duty called, and I spent the whole day trailing around after the movie couple, who were very friendly. Adrian had one of the first Kodak

Instamatic Polaroid Land cameras and frightened the wits out of some of the local lads, taking pictures of them dressed up in spear and pipe (and nothing else) and then producing their likeness from his magic box. My day with the Gaynors wound up with dinner at the hotel and I drove them back to the steamer.

By this time bush telegraph had alerted all fifteen of my fellow Brit bachelors and every single one of them was at the hotel partying it up with the two Canadian girls who'd spent the day swimming in the pool and being wined and dined by the pack of wolves. As last arrival on the scene, I was a bit disadvantaged but a combination of perseverance and pig-ignorance got me into the circle. My pal, Ted, and I eventually eliminated the competition, partying with the two Canadian girls through the night. We saw them aboard at dawn and jumped ashore as the gap widened between steamer and jetty (the river full of crocs and hippos).

The much-delayed sequel to the story is that I again caught up with the attractive brunette six years later in Toronto and we've now been married thirty-five years.

Sincerely,
Alec Herbert

Dear Mr. Black:

My neo-Luddite, nearly pathological aversion to Mr. Bell's infernal device has in no way abated since the last time I was moved to respond to one of your requests for personal experience tales.

In the late '50s I met two remarkable people in Jackson Hole, Wyoming: Archie and Pat Teater. Anyone familiar with the Grand Teton area knows Archie's magnificently realistic paintings.

I suppose I'd be within your definition of brushes with greatness if I wrote about Archie, but we became friends and while I recognize the privilege I had in knowing him, my subject is another.

One afternoon he invited me to come to a party at their winter home in Ketchum, Idaho, just over the mountain.

The house was immense and I didn't see all the guests as they arrived although I recognized a number of well-known faces in the crowd of strangers. Shy and brought up to respect people's privacy, I spoke to no one until I'd been introduced.

I saw a man sitting alone in a dark alcove off the kitchen.

For a moment I was hesitant. Then in a gulp, stride and stammer I was bleating my name like an hysterical sycophant.

He was big. He was massive. He was solid and silent and still. His head came up. His eyes were red and wide and wet.

He looked past me.

His eyes sank again to his drink.

"Uhn. Mmurpmph," he said.

"Beg pardon," I said.

"Hmm. Brnff," he said.

I said, "I'm pleased to meet you, Mr. Hemingway."

Then I moved away into the main room where Burl Ives was starting another song.

Take care,
Ken Jon Booth

February 8, 1993

Dear Arthur:

I forget who it was that was talking about being sociable at parties etc. You both said that it's very difficult to make contact on an elevator.

Now I'm an extremely unsociable person but I have had one sociable contact on an elevator, and since this is one more than most people I thought I'd share it with you.

Seven or eight years ago this fall I went to New York to hear the Metropolitan Opera and I was staying at the Empire Hotel, which is just across the road from the Lincoln Centre. Since then the Empire has done considerable renovating and priced itself right out my category but at the time it was a pleasantly inefficient, somewhat ramshackle place. I must have been up on the tenth or eleventh floor and the elevators were slow. I was going down one morning for breakfast and when I got on there were two other people on — an immaculately dressed woman and an eccentrically dressed man (or perhaps I should say bohemianly dressed — if that's a word). Anyway, he was trying to sing "All the Way" to this woman and he couldn't remember the words. I have this sort or curse/blessing. I am blessed with an exceptionally good memory of the words of songs and cursed with being totally incapable of carrying a tune. When my kids were younger and still at home they always managed to stay out of the house on November 11th because by the time the day was over I'd have gone through Vera Lynn's entire repertoire. When I stepped onto the elevator the man asked me if I knew the words to "All the Way,"

190

and when I told him I did he asked me if I would recite them to him. So all the way down, and it was a very slow elevator, I would speak the line and he would sing it. When we got off he thanked me profusely, did a little pirouette and launched into a chorus of "Autumn in New York." I don't think this proves anything except that New Yorkers are crazy.

I love your program and I'd love to win your book.

All the best in the new building,
Sheilagh Geer

Dear Arthur:

I realize this is very late for your feature on "lost & found" stories but this tale is so recent that I have been too thrilled to sit still enough to write!

In October I lost my wedding rings — I "accidently donated" them to our church garage sale. (But that is another story!) I searched high and low around town and offered a reward in the local papers. This search produced two strange phone calls and a ring that wasn't mine (but that is another story too!). Eventually I gave up my search and just had to accept the situation. Then, Christmas Eve, as we were returning from looking at Christmas lights, we found a paper bag on our doorstep and inside were my rings! — no note, no card, no explanation of any sort, just an anonymous Merry Christmas! I don't mind telling you that I bawled my eyes out.

Two weeks have passed and I still have moments of surprise when I "notice" that I am wearing my rings again. Not only am I delighted to have my rings back, I am happy to think of how good someone else must feel about themselves for the lovely Christmas memory they gave me!

Lorraine Baker

Dear Arthur:

I just finished having a struggle with your answering machine (in both official languages) so I thought I would get my experience down on paper instead.

Coincidence (for want of a better explanation)

Several years ago we were asked to make a long-term commitment to foster a toddler with Down syndrome. This request came at a time when we had just moved into our unfinished new home in a new community and were beginning a completely new lifestyle . . . Nowhere on our master plan was a young child, much less a handicapped one, included. The caseworker requested that we visit the nursery stimulation program she was enrolled in to observe her before making up our minds "against" taking on this responsibility.

My husband and I did go to the nursery class and had just returned home and were sitting at our table with a cup of coffee weighing all the pros and cons of our decision when there was a knock at our door . . .

The couple who were there had never been to our home before (or since) — they were summer neighbours of a relative at their cottage who we had met just casually before. They had been in the area and had heard that we had moved in and decided to "go by our place" to have a look, but something compelled them to drive in and say hello.

The first coincidence was that this couple had a young

daughter the same age as our niece and they were close "summer" friends and this daughter had been to our cottage — on the same lake — several times. This girl's name was the same as the little child we were considering!!!!

It was due to this coincidence that I told this lady about the decision we were making and how strange that they happened to drop in just then. In the process of the conversation it was mentioned that we were unprepared — having long since given up all our baby equipment — and they told us that they always had a crib ready for grandchildren visits and for some reason they now had two at their place and I was welcome to the use of one if I wished.

We did decide to take the child and took them up on their offer of the crib. When we were setting up the crib in our home we realized that this crib was one that we had given away *ten years* before!!

It was this realization that gave me a special feeling that this commitment was "right" for our family despite the extra hassles etc. and we have never regretted our decision.

Stephanie is now a teen — we adopted her when she was six — and through our experiences with her we have learned to "stop and smell the roses" and met many new and special friends . . . our entire lives greatly enriched.

Yours truly,
Caryl Oja

P.S. Love your weekly column in the North Shore *Sentinel* . . . can certainly relate to your Sauna memories — being married to a Finn.

March 5, 1991

Dear Arthur:

I've enjoyed your show for a long time, and it's a pleasure indeed when I can sit at my sewing machine on a sunny Saturday morning with "Basic Black" to keep me company!

I find so many of your interviews intriguing and entertaining, but my curiosity was really piqued by a comment from one of the two left-handed fellows you interviewed March 2. He commented that even the flush on the john was on the wrong side to flush when you're sitting down! The thought immediately flashed through my mind: Who flushes the john sitting down?

That question then led to others like it — many of these raised in my circle of intimates when we are pondering life's imponderables: Why does women's underwear cost more than men's? And why can't women get functional wool socks for the same price as men (never mind the designer logo)? And the question that has haunted me for some years now . . . Who supports the men's pyjama industry? Though in my circle our research is severely limited, none of us could identify many out and out supporters. Is this the real reason for Free Trade — to support an otherwise hopeless business, to open up the vistas of the great U. S. of A. to pyjama manufacturers in Canada? But if the hardy men of the North are undersubscribers, why would the warm South be interested . . . ? It seems there are no answers, and life is so full of such imponderables. Maybe you could ask your phone-in folks to collect a list of such questions.

Whatever you do, keep on talkin'!

Kathryn Guthrie

195

November 23, 1991

Greetings, Mr. Black!

I have been listening to your radio program for many years and truly enjoy it. I have never written to you and felt compelled to share with you a most embarrassing moment which I experienced a few years ago. If it is not suitable for radio, then I hope you may get a bit of laughter from it. It's a true story!

Many years ago, I bowled on a small mixed league and at year's end, we had our usual bowling banquet for presentation of trophies and of course, food and drink. I had second thoughts about attending, since I had, on the previous day, put on a large feed of sauerkraut and made an absolute pig of myself. I knew that for the next twenty-four hours, I would be quite rancid.

When I arrived at the lounge with my girlfriend, I felt the worst was over. The master of ceremonies was presenting the trophies, after we had completed our meal, and was thanking all for a successful year, when I felt a sudden pressure from within . . .

The plot now thickens.

I was sitting between my girlfriend and her mother. About seventy-five people were in the room. My main concern was to avoid any noise . . . so I gripped the bottom of my chair, trying to act nonchalant, and hoping to muffle any sound that might escape.

That move backfired, literally speaking, and I broke wind in a most convincing manner, sounding somewhat like the repetition of an AK-47 assault rifle!

I just wanted to crawl under the carpet, and needless to say, my girlfriend was quite browned off . . . no pun intended.

Love your show!!!!

Sincerely,
Laurie Blanchard

December 8, 1991

Dear Arthur Black:

I have listened to your show forever and I — well, not exactly forever, but pretty darn close, and I just wanted to say — well, okay, maybe not close to forever, but sort of in the general area. Actually, I haven't listened to your show even remotely near to forever.

But I have listened to your show for a very long time and I just — well, sort of for a long time, more sort of a longish time, really. Now that I think about it, it's been an off and on, now and then, here and there, sort of . . . time . . . or . . . uhm . . . something . . .

Dear Arthur Black:

I have listened to your show.

Sincerely yours,
Christof Wyss

(Well, sort of sincerely . . . maybe less than truly sincerely but almost somewhere in the same ball-park-or-at-least-out-in-the-parking-lot-though-not-exactly-next-door-but-at-least-in-the-same-general-city-or-province-and-almost-certainly-in-the-same-country-perhaps to something nearly positive . . .)

January 16, 1993

Dear Arthur:

We live in the wilderness 100 miles north of the Yukon River near the Yukon Territory border with Alaska. Your show is our favorite on the radio and that's saying a lot.

We have an AM radio hooked up to a solar panel, car battery, and a thousand feet of wire for an antenna. That is how we hear you, as the nearest station is more than 500 miles away. We usually hear you on CBC Yukon (Whitehorse) or CBC Western Arctic (Inuvik) or sometimes Yellowknife or Grand Prairie. We hear stations from all over the world, so you can see how much we love you as your program is our favorite. We have no TV, VCR, or any other entertainment except audio tapes. In fact, we only get mail two or three times a year. The nearest town is 150 miles away. All our mail comes by bush plane that lands on the river in front of our cabin. Our nearest neighbors are twenty-two miles away. We see them about eight times a year.

Sometimes we go for six months without seeing another human soul. That is why we rely upon your program to keep us informed of how the barbarians are living.

If we don't win your book, please tell us how we can order one. We guarantee that we will read it. *We read everything we can get our hands on.*

Our thirteen dogs loved your moose calls. Of course they'll howl at anything. Tim has a great wolf call, if you ever need his expertise to join your chorus — twelve years of living in the woods has given him lots of experience.

Your cross-border radio swipers,
Jeanette & Tim Henry

List of Contributors

Debbie Sayles	Apsley, Ont.
Frances Fryza	North York, Ont.
Stewart Hyson	Saint John, N.B.
Cynthia Ellis	Kelowna, B.C.
Jean Rath	Orleans, Ont.
Diane, Cyril, and Amelia Smeltzer	Larry's River, N.S.
C. K. Dresser	Toronto, Ont.
Dorothy Jones	Victoria, B.C.
Ken and Irene Lloyd	Didsbury, Alta.
Heidi Klein	Ottawa, Ont.
Marny Forrest	Petawawa, Ont.
Irene	Salmon Arm, B.C.
Janice Delaney	Nepean, Ont.
Jean Greenough	Edmonton, Alta.
Randy Germain	Toronto, Ont.
Ethel McNeill	Kingston, Ont.
Al & Willma Slater	Victoria, B.C.
Lee Davis	Maple Ridge, B.C.
Arthur Peters	Vancouver, B.C.
Kathleen Ten Wolde	Quesnel, B.C.
Sherlee Aho	Wawa, Ont.
Derek Wilson	Winnipeg, Man.
Glenness Milette & Dale Baldwin	Elko, B.C.
Mary McSweeny	Nanaimo, B.C.
Chris Dubelaar	Edmonton, Alta.
Steven Dang	Vancouver, B.C.
Stephen Branch	Fredericton, N.B.
Harry Lane	Mayne Island, B.C.
Michael J. Bakerpearce	Kenilworth, Ont.
June Holloway	Kingston, Ont.
Joan Fischer	Histowel, Ont.
Allan Goddard	Almonte, Ont.
Clyde Gilmour	Toronto, Ont.
Marian Robertson	Bright's Grove, Ont.
Hugh McMillan	Chatham, Ont.
Al Lewis	Dugald, Man.
Colin Reid	Winlaw, B.C.
Anne Kuntz	Windsor, Ont.
George Cadogan	Guelph, Ont.
Claire Mowat	Port Hope, Ont.
Berrel Garshowitz	Toronto, Ont.
Renée McKee	Lund, B.C.
Jean Woods	Regina, Sask.
Richard S. Mowry	Timmins, Ont.
Ollie Hillman	Winnipeg, Man.
M. A. Gould	Consort, Alta.
Mary Collins	Fenlon Falls, Ont.
Barbara Butler	Cambridge Bay, N.W.T.
Mary Waldbauer	Terrace, B.C.

Christopher Whitehead	Ottawa, Ont.
Denise J. Galloway	Picton, Ont.
Paddy Muir	Halifax, N.S.
Tom	Sydney, N.S.
Linda Bruce	Yellowknife, N.W.T.
Michele Kerschbaumer	Kingston, Ont.
Lindi Pierce	Bonfield, Ont.
Dennis Peters	Orleans, Ont.
Peter R. Wooding	Edmonton, Alta.
Arleane Ralph	Whitby, Ont.
Susan Rysar	Romaino, B.C.
Nancy Crozier	Toronto, Ont.
Mona Pachal	Winnipeg, Man.
Jim Blackburn	Hamilton, Ont.
Geoff Snow	Paris, Ont.
Leslie G. Gratton	Saskatoon, Sask.
Roberto Rouget	Barry's Bay, Ont.
Keith Matheson	Powell River, B.C.
Michael Nitsch	Hastings, Ont.
Rick McConnell	Regina, Sask.
Helen Murphy	Delta, B.C.
Chris Denholm	Toronto, Ont.
Sara Brearley	Coquitlam, B.C.
Don Clark	Dartmouth, N.S.
Pat Fuller	Gabriola Island, B.C.
Jennifer Smith	Halifax, N.S.
Denis Beaudoin	Montreal, P.Q.
Nicky Marchese	Hamilton, Ont.
Sydney B. Turner	Thunder Bay, Ont.
Susan Johnson	Tavistock, Ont.
Alice Clements	Coleman, P.E.I.
Nancy L. Tegart	Windermere, B.C.
Maurice Montreuil	Winnipeg, Man.
Margaret Sangster	Victoria, B.C.
Ronald J. MacDonald	Sydney, N.S.
Pauline M. Berrey	Salmon Arm, B.C.
Betty Gaos	Flinton, Ont.
Ray Marco	Medicine Hat, Alta.
Christine Pike	Waseca, Sask.
Wayne Peters	Winnipeg, Man.
Anne Lloyd	Gloucester, Ont.
Paul Tennant	Vancouver, B.C.
Tony Jenkins	Barriefield, Ont.
Alec Herbert	Winnipeg, Man.
Ken Jon Booth	Prince Rupert, B.C.
Sheilagh Geer	Pine Falls, Man.
Lorraine Baker	Kelowna, B.C.
Caryl Oja	Richards Landing, B.C.
Kathryn Guthrie	Fort Frances, Ont.
Laurie Blanchard	Salisbury, N.B.
Christof Wyss	Montreal, P.Q.
Jeanette & Tim Henry	Eagle, Alaska